Dear Leigh,

Great to meet you on this amazing journey of yours! Stay in touch as I'm looking forward to reading yours.

All the best,

Jordan.

DARK
NECESSITIES

A PSYCHOSPIRITUAL GUIDE TO LIFE AND THE LIVING

This edition first published in 2025 by Maverick MacLire Books.

Offices at:

Maverick MacLire Books

9 Upper Badcall,

Scourie,

Lairg

IV27 4TH

ISBN: 9798306958620

Imprint: Independently published

Cover design and illustration by: Anze Ban Virant

Interior art and design by the author

Typeset in Baskerville and American Typewriter

Printed by Amazon Kindle Direct Publishing KDP

For Katie,

I don't know how I found you, I've stopped questioning why I deserve to have the support and love you give me. My life, my children, true happiness and now this... thank you.

Contents

Preface..7
Introduction..10

The Book
Animysticism..16
Spirit Animals..30
Compassion..48
Fear Of Intelligence..................................63
Fear Not..70
We Are All Connected..................................85
Why A Shaman..96
Sigma Stigma...111
The System...127
Healing Tools..146
Hello Darkness My Old Friend.........................161
Becoming 'The Witness' Not 'The Worry'...............174
Beware The 'Agent'...................................184
Conclusion For Now...................................201

Additional Help
Four Directions Blessings............................207
Morning Prayers......................................218
The Author...223
Acknowledgements.....................................228
Further Reading......................................230

Preface

Most of what you are about tc

from a lifetime of human interaction and an awful lot of

reading and research. This book was inevitable. I have

been writing stories, prose and music since I was 11

years of age. Now in my 43rd year, what had started as

regular blogs has become a re-ignition of creativity;

often feeling like automatic writing.

I do not write from notes, I write and edit

simultaneously. If you read any quotations they are

added not as an after thought but to better explain and

hopefully instil some confidence in you the reader; that

my words are not flippant and meaningless. That my

thoughts are not original but are shared with a collective

of far more brilliant and accomplished souls than myself.

I had a childhood like everyone else, it was mine and

mine alone. It was not until I was of an age to discuss

my early years and share experiences with other souls

that I realised just how polarised an experience it was. I

cannot deny that I would not wish it upon anyone else

but it has certainly shaped me in ways that I am truly grateful for. I hold no grudges for those that have abused positions of responsibility regarding my childhood. I have no friendships or family in my present circle that do not support my life completely.

It is for those that have quietly supported me that I have the most gratitude towards. It is my connection to nature that has given me the compassion I need to forgive myself and others who have caused me suffering. I honestly would not change a thing…

"If there is no struggle, there is no progress. Every step toward the goal of justice requires sacrifice, suffering, and struggle". Martin Luther King, Jr.

I am a writer who is fortunate enough to not suffer from 'writers block'. Only because if I am not feeling creative then I will just focus those two hours of my day on another passion. I have jobs and commitments outside of my creative endeavours. I am a Holistic Counsellor, a Shamanic Healer, an Animystic, a Bard, a Home Educator, a Crofter and I run a small Retreat. It sounds

exhausting! And sometimes it is, but this is the life I chose and I am fortunate enough to be able to live where I do and the way I want to without financial or emotional support from outside of our wee world.

Without this bubble I would not have had the space to dive even deeper into my dark side. Now I will take a rest for a while and ponder my next adventure. I fear this is the first of many books.

Aside from the gift of being a husband to my infinitely generous wife and my wonderfully feral but angelic children; if I can touch just one soul with the words within this book then that will be the greatest gift of all. Please enjoy and please reach out. You can find me in Badcall Bay in the remote North Western Coast of the Scottish Highlands: www.badcallbayretreat.com

Introduction

"Coming out to the light of day
We got many moons that are deep at play
So I keep an eye on the shadow's smile
To see what it has to say."
- Dark Necessities, Red Hot Chili Peppers.

Dark Necessities is not just the title of my book; if I ever do an audible version of this (fingers crossed) I would do the narrating myself and right now the narrative would be accompanied with permission by the Red Hot Chili Peppers song of the same name.

It became very apparent that all of my thoughts and feelings towards the shadow side of my own ego have already been expressed in so many forms by numerous artists, authors, doctors and philosophers of the past and present. This book is an amalgamation of my thoughts and current theories concerning my journey and relationships with individuals and society in this life thus far.

It was not an accident, it was an inevitability.

I am addicted to words and the power of wisdom and knowledge. Not in becoming more knowledgable or powerful, but in the infinitely repeatable journey that we can all take when tackling a new concept for the first time. Unlike the taking of a highly addictive drug where you are always trying to match that first hit (as I am told); the deep dive of researching and developing an understanding for a new concept and then the excitement of putting pen to paper (so to speak), is for me, as equally satisfying as it is rewarding every single time.

Halfway through this wonderful experience of writing my first book I realised what I was actually doing. It was not that it had no purpose from the start, it was just so automatic and energetic that I literally had no time to pause and do what humans love doing the most; give it a name.

This book is about navigating through a society that has not just lost community in its literal meaning as a collective, but has had the power of self-exploration replaced by a self-policing tenacity that enjoys breaking down the will of free-thinkers with such hunger that only the brave dare speak out.

It is the witness and the observer of behaviours from within and without. It is written with soul and the intention to bring awareness or an awakening to those who may be on a path of wisdom.

If it is not for you then please pass it on or put it down. It may not be the right time or that time may have passed.

"You don't know my mind
You don't know my kind
Dark necessities are part of my design
Tell the world that I'm falling from the sky
Dark necessities are part of my design".
- Dark Necessities. Red Hot Chili Peppers.

If you take this journey with me I promise you one thing, you will be witness to deep honesty and a connection to Spirit that has been cultivated for many years. For that is the only real explanation I can find for much of the how and what I have written.

"I know that I know nothing" (Plato) and I am okay with that. It is witnessing the behaviour of groups and individuals. It is witnessing my own feelings and thoughts that has driven me to search for answers. Dip into this journey with me, it has been lonely at times and now I am ready to share my insights; I hope that one day I get to experience yours too...

Try and see through the darkness in these words only then can they illuminate a path for you.

"Casting aside other things, hold to the precious few; and besides bear in mind that every man lives only the present, which is an indivisible point, and that all the rest of his life is either past or is uncertain. Brief is man's life and small the nook of the earth where he lives; brief, too, is the longest post humous fame, buoyed only by a succession of poor human beings who will very soon die and know little of themselves, much less of someone who died long ago." Marcus Aurelius.

The Book

Animysticism

Our recent past shrouded in darkness.

A darkness dressed in a white robe.

They feed on your fear, obedience and will.

Nature watches...

Her eternal beauty unfathomable to mortal minds,

She calls out to us, she sends her birds.

She sends spirits within bodies to inspire and inform.

All the while the darkness dressed in white lingers,

Snapping at the flocks' heels if they stray too far,

Shrouding them in ignorance, promising redemption.

Nature watches...

She calls out to us, she sends the wind.

They stay inside their castles shrouded in darkness.

The wise man listens as she whips his face,

He smiles as she flies overhead.

He thanks her for her wisdom, and her patience.

He turns and sees them, shrouded in darkness.

They see this madman with his smile on his face.

They feel his joy and question this place.

Nature watches...

Animism - "The belief that all natural things, such as plants, animals, rocks and thunder, have spirits and can influence human events" - Cambridge Dictionary.

I would like to think I have no rigid beliefs. I pride myself on having fluidity of thought and am always willing to hear another perspective. Perhaps I believe this but whatever teachings cross my path and sometimes guide my beliefs, I have always been and will always be an Animist. So, I guess I am not as open-minded as I would like to think.

Animism is the belief that every atom, every molecule, that absolutely anything with physicality carries a form of consciousness and therefore has purpose and should be respected. It is the belief that any emotion, non-physical feeling, spirit or entity also has consciousness and a soul.

Before we move along, what is a soul to me the author? It is the immaterial part of us that is immortal and separate from our human bodies. It gives life to the body and is the seat of our personality, intellect, will and emotions. It is what remains when the body dies. It is who we are in every life in every body (or avatar) and who we return to when we exist as Spirit between lives, in different bodies, with different identities.

The soul is relatively easy to understand. This idea resonates. Intuitively there seems to be truth behind this theory.

What I do not understand is whether there is such thing as a subjective consciousness. Is there an infinite amount of consciousness or just a singular consciousness that is in everything experiencing everything but essentially the same thing? Are we just one soul fragmented into an infinite number of egos living and experiencing the all? Big questions, let's move on and let our subconscious minds do the work on that (or just forget it completely!).

Everything that happens around you is a reflection of the energy you omit. Humans carry a unique ability (arguably an ability shared with only a few other species on our planet) of manifesting pretty much everything you can imagine through the manipulation of energy and our own consciousness.

If everybody on Earth was aware of their true potential without doing a serious amount of Shadow work to become comfortable with the dark side of their personality; forget World War 3, we would literally create a biblical 'hell on Earth'.

As a researcher of the Gnostics of old and the 'you-tubers' of new, as a filterer of the 'chaff' (there is far too much!), I find it hard not to believe that other off-world beings (higher beings, more evolved entities or 'aliens') are not purposefully guarding the rest of the cosmos from our dangerously powerful and untamed manifestations. As Carl Jung clearly stated in most of his work we are the creators of our own evil, humans are the potential nightmare, it is not external to us, it is us. Therefore, Animism is not just the practice of many spiritual healers and indigenous tribes, it is a method of personifying 'all' that there is around us without having to understand the 'all'. It takes our fear away and gives life and respect to everything we see and feel including ourselves and our feelings. Most importantly it connects us to everything that is around us without having to give it a scientific name and study it without honouring its spirit.

During the Iron Age of Celtic Britain, the Britons (as they were called) did not practice Shamanism. The Bards, Druids and Healers practiced Animism.

The Druids were the early scientists, philosophers, teachers, astrologers, lawyers and decision makers. They were keepers of wisdom and the educators of this wisdom. They were also keepers of secrets and were wise enough to hold back certain wisdom teachings from those who would abuse it.

The Bards were the singers, the dancers, the musicians, the spell casters and the communicators. They could make you laugh and cry, they could lift a room and set a mood appropriate for an occasion. They would dance your death while singing of your life and your adventures. They would help your soul as it transitioned into the realm of spirit. They would help your family and loved ones as well. They were the "mental librarians of there tribe." - Stella Marie.[1] They believed in

------

[1] Check out her YouTube channel for more information on traditional Celtic spiritual practices. Her channel: 'Stella Marie | Starlit Stories.

reincarnation, our eternal souls, moving between spiritual realms and shapeshifting. Are you starting to see similarities with indigenous forms of Shamanism still found in our world today?

Whatever their instrument: a drum, a fiddle (of sorts), these Celts were connected to Source[2] through music and movement. Contrary to popular belief our ancient practices were not completely wiped out of the history books by religion. The Bards wrote down a lot of their prose and thoughts and this is readily available in book form today. 'Irish Bardic Poetry and Rhetorical Reality' by Michelle O'Riordan holds a lot of this wisdom and most importantly it is pre Christian. Everything written after the Christian spiritual take-over was essentially written by Monks who would have removed any real spiritual wisdom from any of these texts. As individuals they were probably wisdom seekers themselves. As followers under the command of the Church, they would have been under the watchful eye and strict rules of their 'higher ups'. The Christian Church has A LOT

---

[2] 'Source' - some people use this term instead of 'god'. It refers to a divine or a higher power, also known as the 'Creator'.

to answer for and some of us still find it hard to forgive this new-age dogmatic control system. At least we can be honest about our feelings without fear of being burnt to death in front of (and by) our community. It still does not take away the fact that many Medicine Women were burnt to death for herbalism and other healing practices. They were murdered for their connection to Spirit and their practice of Animism. The Church was afraid of their power and how their communities relied upon them for healing and wisdom. The Church wanted the power and so it taught its followers that the only way to redemption was through Jesus and the only way to access him was through the Church. They enforced the idea that the only humans who were truly connected to Jesus and God were the priests and the only entity worth your worship was Jesus (arguably a Shaman himself). Any deviation would be punished severely. It was not a spiritual practice it was a dystopian nightmare created by a powerful system of control.

The Bards and Druids were the bridge between humanity and Spirit, the Church burnt the bridge and made the gap too wide to safely cross. They set spikes and quicksand to catch deviants who strayed from the 'holy' path.

Sadly, nothing has changed. They are still on a recruiting drive and I think it is still absolutely pointless trying to have an intelligent debate with a devout Christian (please prove me wrong). Verses will be thrown at you, they will bless you and pray that Christ redeems your evil ways whilst I quietly whisper protective runic spells and give them a taste of their own medicine. If you obey this 'off-world' God who separates humanity from nature, places humans above all of 'Gods Creatures' on 'His' egocentric pedestal, you are not 'spiritual', you are in a dogmatic cult. Who is this cruel God who demands your attention and will punish your insubordination with eternal damnation? Even if you didn't worship him through the innocence of say, being born on a desert island without a copy of the Bible or an education to read it, do you still believe in eternal damnation? I have read 'Dante's Inferno' and I loved it as a work of literature and a study of our lives and the popular need for redemption, that is all.

My belief is that true hell exists on Earth and is subjective; you create it yourself, you are not thrown into it by some unforgiving, all encompassing, bearded man-God with a bad temper and an immeasurable ego. Our souls are infinite but your suffering does not have to be. I was born into a Christian family, my Mother was a Protestant, my Father a Catholic. His Father who fought in the Royal Navy in the Second World War passed on some wisdom (although he passed over before my birth). I am grateful for his life and have continued to have the gift of his wisdom through spiritual connection. Grandad Bill was a devout Catholic as were many men whom the Church commanded. The patriarchal Church system required all men to lead their wives and children and I'm sure my Grandad did this in his own Glaswegian way, with a little jig in his step (he was well known for his dancing!). It was after the birth of seven children, and another two that died during childbirth that William decided enough was enough. He spoke to his local priest about contraception. This I believe would have been in the 1960's although I am not certain. He was removed from the Church for refusing to have any more children and I imagine he practiced his own version of worship from his busy, warm home instead of the cold walls of the local church.

He escaped the Church! He also survived being on board three ships that were sunk by the Nazis. His commanding officers were unsure whether he was the luckiest seaman alive or a bad omen for any ship he was aboard. He was ordered to fight for the army infantry during the infamous D-Day landings and the weeks and months of the final horrors of that war. It was being shot in the leg that potentially saved his life. It was not a German who shot him though, it was a Frenchman. He had 'found' a chicken near a farm and half starved, took it for sustenance. His act of bravery to help feed his friends also meant that I could be here today writing this book. I have a lot of gratitude, respect and love for this man, I always have. I was always fascinated with the Grandfather I never met. His strength, courage, will and tireless disruption towards rigid systems of control have been passed to me through his stories and genetic lineage. We make our own paths through life (if we choose not to be part of a flock). I am my own shepherd and my equal, my wife and I do not control our children, we set an example by loving them and everything around us with compassion and respect. Even the people whom we do not like and disagree with, they are shown this compassion and our children bear witness.

If they turn out to follow our path of Animism then so be it. Whatever path they choose we will always be available for guidance without smothering their experiences with worry and fear. One thing is for sure and will never change; we will not let any Church or any religion near our children. Once we believe they have enough control of their own minds to not be susceptible to fear based dogma, then we will let them explore all avenues. This is not 'helicopter parenting', this is protecting our children from ignorance and evil.

I have compassion for religious followers, especially the ones that feel that they have to explain themselves to me. You see I am sure about my feelings towards the Church and I have read the Bible, I have been to a religious military College, I have sung for the late Queen in St. Pauls Cathedral three times on Remembrance Sunday. I know Christianity. I know that this 'new age', 'accepting of others' movement is just a last attempt to hypnotise weaker minds and worm their way into our homes again. Stay strong, by all means turn to Jesus the ascended master, the Shaman, but not the redeemer. There is no need for redemption, only exploration and connection. You have an ego because you are having a subjective experience, do not be dragged into a life of oppression, it is madness. Be the 'weird' one who explores all avenues, do not just follow your parents paths, stand on your own two feet, use your own mind, and draw from the abundance of human experience that is available. You be you.

This is Animysticism. It is the essence of what I write, the undertone of Animism and the compassion towards everything that rises above feelings and reactivity. It is my version of Gnosticism, the version that resonates with me. What resonates with you?

Read this chapter again if you feel attacked by any religious types. It has helped me to alchemise my anger towards bigotry. I was seething when writing some of this and distinctly calm at the end. I do not think it is healthy or right to deny the horrors of humanities past. There is enough horror in our present.

There is a protective bind rune that is behind the text on this page. It is a very powerful protective spell. The thorn and Giants' energy of the unforgiving Thurisaz, calmed by the introspective invisibility cloak of Algiz; both brought together by inviting only the just and the brave with the wisdom of community with Eiwaz (the yew tree). As a family we have this bind rune on our gates and our exterior doors. I rarely work with the rune Thurisaz. If you know your runes you will understand why. It is aggressive and unforgiving. It has a tendency to fly back to the sender, hence why it is also Thors rune and represents Mjolnir the infamous hammer that is infused with the power of the Giants.

Our Celtic ancestors used these runes for hundreds of years as an Alphabet, for magik and for divination. They were part of our culture then and I have a passion for their wisdom as they are just as useful a tool in the modern world.

If you want to learn a lot more about them and how they can help you please reach out to us. If you can wait, I am halfway through my own explanation of the runes as a Celtic practitioner of their wisdom. The book I release (in 2025) will be small enough to keep your attention but full of my experience with this magik. There will be enough explanation for you to start your own relationship with them. You see, as an Animist I believe the runes have a spirit and a consciousness. This belief gives power to the process and honours them. They work with me, I do not work for them.

You can apply Animism to everything you do and connect with. That is why it is such a beautiful and rewarding practice. I honour my ancestors by following these teachings. I do not feel obliged to do so but my very being resonates with gratitude when I live this way.

Spirit Animals

A gentle nudge, a tingling on my arm or neck,
Raven lends me a cheeky smile and jogs my mind.
I see through the words, read between the lines,
Their feelings, emotions all becomes clear.
The trickster matches tone and melts into obscurity.

A flutter in my heart, an unwelcome feeling,
Wolf holds me, that familiar warmth and scent.
Letting go of old behaviours no longer needed.
A blanket of familiarity wraps around me,
I feel protected from within and without.

A sudden clarity, a crisp, clear communication,
Kingfisher calls me to the waters edge for quiet
contemplation.
The messages are clear, It's time to take the plunge,
Into that project, into the unknown.
To trust in your instincts is to trust in Mother Nature.

Sometimes we all love to jump on a new trend. How many times have you done a 'quick quiz' to find out your Intelligence Quotation or what your Spirit Animal or Guide is? These tests are becoming readily available and are pushed in front of our digital lives through marketing and advertising campaigns. Although I find the advertising world to be intrusive and dark; It is a promising sign for humanity that the money men can see a population getting more and more in touch with their spiritual routes and alternative medicines. It is a shame that the tests are absolute nonsense but if interest in the esoteric is sparked then it's a step in the right direction…

This is my insight into what these guides represent in terms of Animism, Shamanism and how important this was to our ancestors for survival and for our healthy living today.

On my shamanic journey of remembering my souls purpose in this life, I have had many journeys into non physical realms. The metaphysical universe is as real to me as the three dimensional one. I had visited these realms in my dreams as a child, not fully realising their significance at the time. Only when learning to navigate them as an adult did I feel and sense the similarities with my childhood dreams. I am forever fascinated by and full of gratitude that I have awakened to these realms, to being a spiritual being in a human incarnation. It turns out that this is not my first rodeo as a human. Past life regressions have taken me back at least 2000 years to a life as a chief prison guard for the Roman Empire (as a European Celt not as a Roman). Needless to say I have had to work on some karmic lessons from that particular incarnation!

When I do 'journey work' or healing for others I will always call upon my guides for support and guidance. It can be very daunting to try and navigate the realms on your own. Thankfully we are never truly alone…

We all have spirit guides, whether they are ancestral, celestial, angelic or represented by an animal. Even if you do not see them or have not 'met' them in your spiritual journey as of yet, they have been with you since before your birth, guiding you. Your benevolent spirits will heed your call and give you guidance if you know how to ask for it. They actively help you even if you are unaware of them. They are a part of your personality in this life and a part of your higher self, your over-watching soul that transcends your ego as a human.

There are (in many shamanic traditions) three realms to the metaphysical. The Upper, Middle and Lower. Each realm represents an aspect of a souls journey and is home to a specific part of us personified by an animal and its particular characteristics.

On my life journey I have been fortunate enough (through mentorship) to find an animal guide to help me navigate each of these. When people meet their guides (or are made aware what and who they are by a shamanic practitioner) there may be a rush to google what the spiritual meaning is behind the animal. I have been taught that to build a true connection you must try to study the actual behaviour of said animal in the wild (not in a zoo). If you cannot physically see the animal (for example if it is not native to you or not visible or known to exist in our three-dimensional realm such as a

Dragon or a Unicorn), then watch a documentary or film relevant to them. Try and see their characteristics, how they hunt, what they eat, how they look after their young or pack. Are they social? Do they migrate with changing weather patterns?

After you have practiced this, now is the right time to search for spiritual references outside of your own observations. I have tried so many different books but through years of my experience, the most accurate book that is easy to work with is 'Animal Spirit Guides' by Steven D. Farmer. This is always my go to, to help understand my clients guides' and my own. It is also my favourite tool if I see a message in the form of an animal in nature. Animals in our Earth dream will send you messages in the form of synchronicity; once you know how to read these signs you cannot un-see them. Steven Farmer's book not only explains about the animals spirit as a guide but also as a messenger. Not all connections with these sprits are from our specific guides, we are connected to all of nature through Spirit.

I am fortunate to live in an isolated part of the Scottish Highlands so nature is in abundance. The general rule is the number three. If you have three moments in a short space of time where you see the same animal and often in three different ways then this is the synchronicity of a sign or message from Source (Nature, God etc.). You may see an image of a Raven on your phone or screen, at the same time hear or see a Raven above your head or standing in front of you in nature. With your interest sparked but your daily tasks requiring your intention you continue to focus on your worldly duties (your job, your children etc.). It is the third synchronicity that confirms the message; you may see a Raven on a car sticker or an advert on a van… now you know you must intuit the message.

Once you have a good idea about the characteristics of the animal, look inside yourself and see which of these are already embedded in your own personality and which of these you feel you would benefit from mastering. Be honest with yourself, this is absolutely crucial. Do not let your ego tell you that you do not have a shadow side. We are all equally light and dark. If I was truly honest, I would rather be grey than brilliant white or consumed by darkness. We live in duality so embrace it.

It is wonderful that humanity is becoming open to non-dogmatic spiritual practice again but please understand that your ego is what keeps you alive and gives you motivation to breathe. Do not try and become the 'white fluffy' spiritual angelic being. You are a human, life is hard and so it should be. You cannot live in light unless you experience the dark and life throws so many curveballs you will never dodge them all. With this in mind, you must also know that your animal guides hold a dark aspect as well, this is usually the opposite of their more positive characteristics, very similar to flipping a tarot card around to read its reverse meaning.

I will take you through the different realms and my own personal animal spirit companions for this to make better sense. When we refer to an animal guide we refer to its spirit a species, not the individual. For example it is never 'my wolf' or 'the wolf', it is just 'Wolf'.

The Upper Realm - Kingfisher

The Upper Realm or the Angelic Realm is a place of wisdom, love, healing and compassion. It is a place where we may meet 'ascended masters'; beings who have transcended their egos, and have spiritual insight, wisdom, and compassion. We may also meet our ancestors who quite often act as guides to the living if that is the path they have chosen. When journeying this is usually a world above the clouds, think of a typically angelic scene of the Christian Heaven (but without the patriarchal dogma).

The Kingfisher can be found around most of our planet. They are widespread throughout the United Kingdom in the form of the Eurasian/Common Kingfisher; Alcedo atthis. They are a small bird, electric blue and amber with an oversized dagger shaped bill. They are generally shy but may be viewed on an exposed perch over water where they will be hunting for small fish. They are territorial and will defend their territory with vigour. They will form nests in cavities on river banks, these are very well concealed so it is rare to see Kingfisher's when they are caring for their young.

They have featured heavily in different cultures throughout the world. Sometimes they are seen as a good omen and sometimes bad. They are also a part of Greek Mythology which is a good portrayal of monogamous characteristics; The Gods Alcyone and Ceryx who likened themselves to Zeus and Hera, bred the first pair of the mythical birds Halcyon (kingfishers). They died for comparing themselves to the great Olympians but the other Gods compassionately made them into birds and restored them to their seaside habitat that they enjoyed as Gods. The term 'Halcyon days' refers to the seven days on either side of the Winter solstice where they were promised calm sees by the Gods. 'Halcyon days' now refers loosely to calm days at sea or as a general term for peaceful Winter weather.

The connection we have to our spirit guides are deeply personal. In some cultures they are never shared unless with the local Shaman or Medicine Women or Man. I feel it is more important for you to have honest examples of potential guides so I will be as open as I am comfortable with.

The Kingfisher as a guide specifically represents a need to move as North as possible and always by a body of water. The last year saw my family move to the far North of Scotland, our land on a Bay on the waters edge.

They represent an articulate and songlike voice; If I am not talking deep and esoteric you find me singing or creating comical prose with my children.

They represent a value for meditation and a scared space in the home; I do all of my meditation, prayer and writing at 5am in the morning every day in a small cubby type office with my computer and main house alter.

They represent a willing to sacrifice your own needs for those you love; Although I have learnt to not give my energy away to clients and the public without reciprocity, my family are given all of my energy freely. I home educate my eldest daughter with great pleasure. I guess it is not really a sacrifice because I gain so much from the energy I put into my family but I had to really change my way of thinking how society wanted us to behave or perform as a family. The sacrifice was letting go of societal constraints and quite a few supposed friends on the way.

The Middle Realm - Wolf

The Middle Realm is the realm of the ego that is consciousness. Your personality and the physical world in which life co-exists with spirit or is a spirit in a physical form. The purpose of this realm (and perhaps life itself) is to transcend the ego whilst experiencing all that consciousness has to offer. To remember that we are all spirit incarnate, that we all come from source, are still a part of source and will fully return to source when ready to become 'one' again. It can be quite a daunting concept to imagine leaving your ego behind and not existing as the individual that is you. The deeper my

spiritual journey goes the more I realise that this life I
am living is just a tiny fragment of what I truly am.

The concept of infinite experience resonates with my
journey. I have come to believe that we can live multiple
(if not infinite) lifetimes. In some of these we will

remember that time is a construct of the ego and that only the now exists but over an infinite different versions. There is a you that decided to walk a different path to work this morning, a version of you that split from your timeline and is coexisting on its own.

The Wolf is a social animal that lives in a hierarchical pact. They form strong emotional bonds with each other and care for each others needs.

They communicate over long distances by howling. They will howl to assemble their pack, find lost members and defend their territory. It is one of their tricks to move in the darkness whilst howling to mask their numbers.

They are natures endurance hunter. They will stalk their prey for hours, often at night, hunting mostly large mammals like deer and moose. They are well known for their keen sense of smell and their excellent hearing and vision.

This does not mean that I spend my evenings hunting local deer and howling in the woods although that would suit me just fine!

As a power animal the Wolf represents an intuitive sense of social order within family and community; a significant affection for friends and family.

They represent someone who would rather avoid confrontation but will fiercely defend loved ones and themselves whenever necessary.

They represent wisdom teachers and great verbal and non-verbal story tellers; their knowledge comes from actual life experience and not just a formal education.

They represent a shy personality that is at ease with close family and friends but feels energetically drained in more shallow social situations especially if small-talk is on the agenda. I don't think I need to explain this in terms of how it represents myself. Just to confirm though, all of these characteristics are deeply imbedded in my psyche and spirit, the Wolf is one of my old guides.

The Lower Realm - Raven

The Lower Realm or World represents our subconscious mind and the home of various spirits who can become our helpers and protectors, our guides. It is usually where a Shaman may first look when a client has had some 'Power Loss' to try and retrieve that Animal Spirit and guide it back home.

This realm is where many people begin their journey into Shamanism. It is though 'journeying' here you may meet your current Spirit guide and it is not recommended that you stay in this realm for too long without them to guard and guide you.

For me this is a misty forest and jungle dreamworld full of wonder, shape-shifting spirits, animals and is generally at dusk.

Raven embodies ancient wisdom and intuitive guidance. My experience of Raven is it is equally dark and light. A messenger from the spirit realm urging people to embrace their power and transform.

They are shape-shifters as spirit and can be tricksters but as a guide I often feel Raven appears when I need to learn a tough lesson!

In the wild Ravens are super-smart and often playful. Often flipping upside down with closed wings in a sort of dance. They are elusive for weeks and then may suddenly appear, occasionally coinciding with the death of livestock or a wild animal.

Mostly seen in pairs but in the Winter young birds may come together to roost in big groups.

They are excellent hunters and scavengers and mostly eat carrion, insects and small live prey.

They can mimic human voices, make gestures and remember your face so beware how you treat them!

Throughout the world different cultures will have different practices. Some Native American Shamans believe you have nine Spirit Guides other cultures believe you have only 1. I was taught by the Shamans Jay & Kestrel Oakwood ('The Call Of The Shaman' training in Glastonbury) that you have three and although I was already practicing Shamanism before their mentorship, their method resonates with me as it incorporates the three realms I work within. My three guides have become integral to my practice.

I believe that you require different guides at different life stages. They do not disappear but rather they integrate into you fully and create space for new guides with new lessons and new qualities to strive for.

The initial journeys to find these guides are best undertaken with a trained Shamanic practitioner, that is not to say that you cannot try on your own but please use your intuition to guide you! Most journeys start with the imagination. Be patient with yourself, we all see and feel our way through journey work in unique ways. I get a mix of emotions and intuition followed by visual confirmation. Some people have obvious conversations with their guides and ancestors, my messages and visions are far more cryptic and I find the messages have many meanings that take time and further meditation to become clearer. I like to work a bit harder for my answers but am well practiced at deciphering the abstract by this point in my life.

My wife and I love helping people on their spiritual journey. If we offer help or a chance for an esoteric chat then please know it is a genuine offer. Reach out if you have insights or opinions on your own practice. If you are triggered, remember to not take anything personally, you be you. My ancestors have guided me to this point of my journey and I have direct contact with them. If you feel lost and disconnected, reach out, there are many trained and practiced Shamanic practitioners, most of which are fairly easy to find on the internet. Before you go it alone, seek some guidance from a mentor. No matter how far I think I have come I always humble myself with the knowledge that 'I am nothing, I know nothing'.

Compassion

As I witness, bring to light,
My comrades pain, his chest held tight.
It takes me to a memory,
Pushed deep down inside of me.
We take each other in our arms,
Embrace the pain, this cause of harm.
Together now and twice as strong,
We sing our pains and strum our songs.

'Compassion' - The feeling or emotion, when a person is moved by the suffering or distress of another, and by the desire to relieve it; pity that inclines one to spare or to succour." - Oxford English Dictionary.

In a society (in a world) where we are taught from a young age to compete with each other; that success is measured in monetary wealth, what is the use of compassion?

Hopefully you have read the two previous chapters and gained some insight into why true compassion really is our only hope to regain our emotional intelligence as a race…

It is the feeling you may get when you are practicing 'active listening' to another human.

Active listening is a technique that involves paying close attention to what someone is saying, actually listening to them with external and internal silence; not waiting for the chance to have your say, knowing without thinking that your response will come after the speaker has finished.

This practice gives you a chance to be attentive, have reflection and pause before it is your chance to respond. It is also a great pathway to retaining information for later.

The 4 qualities of active listening are:

Paying attention: Try and reduce or ignore your own mental chatter. Focus on the speaker and acknowledge what they are saying.

Show that you are listening: Your posture and your body will be sure signs that you are engaged in active listening. Gestures like nods and smiles will confirm this.

Deferring judgement: Listen to the content without judgement. You are listening, you can process the information when it is your turn to respond.

Responding appropriately: If you do not agree with the speaker, never attack or belittle them. If they do not want advice do not give it to them. You never have to lie and agree with something against your better judgement; but learn to read the room, maybe they just need to let off some steam and your learned advice will just upset them.

The motivation you feel to help someone who is suffering, this is compassion. What a loving and giving aspect to your personality. It is also a selfless trait that can lead you very quickly to burnout. If you constantly give your compassion to others without practicing self-compassion you will feel tired and frustrated by the imbalance of energy.

Have empathy for yourself. If a meeting with someone makes you feel a certain way and that is not how you want to feel; have empathy for that current feeling. Witness it. Do not push it away or down into your shadow. Once you feel comfortable witnessing this feeling you can now explain this behaviour. This is not about removing guilt and justifying anti-social or cruel behaviour. This is about reading the situation, seeing what triggered you in the other person, reading where you felt the feeling and if it reminds you of a past situation or trauma.

We are all on a journey of personal growth. Having deep and uncomfortable feelings are not signs of regression. These are chances to expand and grow. It is not what and how you feel, it is the response you have without the unconscious reaction to the emotion/feeling.

Treat yourself with the unlimited compassion you would treat your favourite pet. If your dog takes food off the table, yes you will say a firm word but then you will let it go. You will not continue to punish the dog day after day for one mistake. Why do we punish ourselves at the instance and then continue to punish ourselves a thousand times? It makes no sense. We have to learn to let go and move on.

Speak kindly about people especially in public. I always feel uncomfortable when drawn into a conversation about someone else. If they (the target) are not present then how can they defend themselves?

It is not right to bolster your negative feelings about someone else by giving strength and value to another persons experiences with the target. How differently would that conversation be if the target was present? I imagine they are standing there actively listening and participating, please try it. All of a sudden, your responses will be softer, more compassionate, less about confirmation bias and more about observation. People behave because of their environment. If they are misunderstood they may feel like they have to defend who they are. I have often seen 'black sheep' of a community that are attacked with whispers and gossip from the shadows just because they are different to everyone else and minding their own business. I do not feel sorry for people or worry about them in any instance. As I have said before, this is taking away their power and is the same as saying 'you do not have the tools to help yourself without my external help or guidance'. Sandra Ingerman (one of my Shamanic mentors) asks us to imagine how it would feel if a football stadium full of people were worried about you. This would not help you it would just alchemise their pity into your self-pity. No one has ever recovered, learnt or healed through self-pity, it is a redundant practice. Wouldn't you rather a crowd of people shouting 'You've got this! You can do it!'? Or even better, support is welcome but wouldn't you rather have the self-awareness and conscious awareness to know that 'you have got this!' Surely that would be a healthy goal to aim for.

I am more focused on the patterns and consistency of the social dynamics of a community than I am on the individuals. There are patterns in everything in nature. If you focus too hard on the smaller picture and take everything personally you will have no compassion for what is actually happening, you will miss the bigger picture.

Something I have been working on with a very close friend; The ability to say sorry and truly mean it.

As children we learn to apologise to gain a positive response to a negative situation. We learn this behaviour before we have learnt to reason about the 'why it was bad behaviour' in the first place. We want our parents or carer to love us and shower us in positive feelings. We will do anything to please them, the ability to reason comes much later.

You are not a child. If you apologise so that you relinquish guilt rather than because you have compassion for the other person/s, then perhaps you should observe this behaviour while it happens. We all make mistakes every day and you are bound to upset someone at some point.

Ask the offended party how you have upset them, practice your 'active listening' techniques and then if you know you are in the wrong look them in the eye, pause for a second and say 'I am sorry'. Follow with a brief but validating blurb of why you are sorry to show how much you were listening and then suggest possible changes you can make to lessen the chance of it happening again. Do not suggest changes they need to make at this point, do not try and defend your ego. If you know you are wrong, you are not giving away your power you are showing that person that you are compassionate, intelligent and kind. What more do you want to be in life and what more would you want from a friend?

In the same way that we should learn to apologise we should also be able to forgive. By holding grudges we are reversing the original offence back to the apologiser. If they have already witnessed and observed their actions, they know they have wronged you and are truly sorry then why would you feel the need to continue the punishment? Even worse if we try and find other people to validate and bolster support for our begrudging behaviour.

Yes there are some situations were we feel people need to be punished punitively or by some other means. Have you ever thought about how forgiveness helps you to let go of negative and heavy feelings and thoughts.

That feeling we get when a 'weight has been lifted', often we have been living with these weights for a long time without even realising the impact they have on our own psychospiritual health. Just let go. Observe, decipher, make adjustments and move on.

When you hear of someones new success how does it make you feel?

Do you genuinely feel joy and celebrate when someone else achieves something positive?

Do you instantly look at your own life and judge them based on what you have and how much you think they deserve?

Being happy for others is about taking pleasure in their good fortune and recognising that their accomplishments are to be admired; they are not a threat to your own achievements.

Positive emotion: Choose to focus on the positive aspects of someone else's success. Try and be genuine when you feel happiness for them. As with most positive practices this will benefit all parties.

No comparison: If you have feelings of jealousy or judgement, use these feelings to drive you to make your life better; perhaps they are highlighting something in the shadows you feel is missing in your own life.

Building relationships: If you show positive support directly to these people you will actively strengthen your relationship and create a network of support. I have witnessed this first-hand, even in business. Competitors have shared their success by giving me guidance. Some people really do like to share their success with other and help their community to thrive. Take note of these souls, they are good ones.

The German word "Freudenfreude" means "joy in joy". Take joy in others success and you are already successful yourself.

Compassion lies at the core of my being. I think I was born with it because I remember feeling it towards my Father when I was a very young child. I remember feeling it towards the Father of one of my friends who was trying to seduce my Mother whilst I stood observing with the other kids outside of our primary school. I have used it to stop myself retaliating with physical violence when others have lost control.

I believe it is crucial to others and to yourself. Without it I think I would be a deeply unhappy human, with it I am a non-judgmental soul.

Nevertheless (and it is not like me to play devil's advocate ;-)), compassion is not a weakness or a willingness to turn the other cheek. You never have to suffer spiritual, physical and mental attacks. I think I have learnt this the hard way with many knocks in all three of these aspects from people in positions of responsibility.

Whether they are parents, teachers, supposed best friends and siblings, you can always walk away. If 'active listening' and many of the other tools are not working, please just walk away. Sometimes a few minutes of slow and steady breathing will be enough for you to gain clarity and composure and perhaps they (the offending party) will benefit as well.

I have mastered the art of walking away, I think it probably looks like I am cold and calculated. I am not. I just do not see the logic behind carrying emotional baggage from bad relationships. The hardest thing I have ever done is walk away from my own family, not the family I have created with my wife but the family I was born into. I do not talk about this very often, it seems to trigger people into a dispassionate state; they often become passive aggressive as if I have personally attacked them and their relationships with their parents and siblings. They are lacking the basic skill of compassion and fortunately I do not need external compassion as I have learnt to have enough for myself.

There is sometimes a feeling of loneliness within the small community of wisdom seekers I have met on this journey. It is not because we have become judgmental or risen above the rest of humanity. It is because without effort we now see patterns in the behaviours of nature and society that we cannot ignore.

Perhaps I can explain it like this; imagine spending 30 years of your life learning every single known and used language on Earth… a time consuming task that requires a serious amount of dedication. All of a sudden, one day you wake up and without any known effort; with an automatic intelligence, you now understand (to some degree) every word that is uttered in every tongue. Not just the words but the hidden context behind them. You can read between the lines.

Many countries have English as a second language, the history of this is because of the Imperialist British colonisation of a large part of the world, often with brutality. There is an academic understanding of a language, pronunciation, grammar, tenses etc. To truly understand the spoken language you have to live around those whom it belongs to. I have met a few non-native (to Britain) people in my life that understand the sarcasm and wit behind the spoken English language. Funnily enough they could not read or write in English but have lived in the UK for 15 years for more. By immersing ourselves in a subject, even if it leaves us isolated until we grasp it's core meaning, that is the key.

"It does not matter how slowly you go, as long as you do not stop". - Confucius.

The word compassion comes from the Latin words 'com' and 'pati', which mean "to bear, suffer". It has been part of the English language since the 14th century. Interesting that Buddhism teaches that all of life is suffering; That it has a cause, an end and a way to end it. A dark necessity that can only be met with growth and learning or it simply does not work.

Compassion is not empathy, it is not the ability to understand and share another's feelings. It is the desire to take action to help someone or ourselves.

Fear of Intelligence

How Intelligence Unintentionally Challenges Mediocrity

Do not question how you think,

And how you feel within this clink.

The others, they will fill the gaps,

They'll wax you lyrical, set up traps.

Just walk away and don't stoop down,

It smells too clever in this town.

Just rise above and smile and wave (boys),

You're not their puppet or their slave.

I became increasingly self-aware that every time I met someone in public who initiated small talk, within a few sentences I would automatically steer the conversation into much deeper context. Rather than trying to display intelligence, I realised this behaviour was born from a fear of dishonesty and a dismissal of any form of gossip where an innocent was being attacked (even the poor weather!). Initially I was attacked for this deepness, jokingly jibed at from being 'too deep' or told to 'lighten up'. This confused me and made me wonder what was wrong with me? Why do they not think and feel like I do?

If this example resonates with you now or in the past I hope my perspective gives you some comfort. It may also lead you to discovering a new and interesting aspect of your personality which I touch on within this book... the 'Sigma' human or 'Intuitive Introvert'.

Why does intellect stir a quiet resentment? The obvious answer is that true intelligence will highlight a lack thereof within others. You do not have to be loud and witty to have intelligence. It is often met with feelings of resentment even by those those who appear to be competitive and financially successful within a social hierarchy. True intelligence will highlight the inadequacies of these people, especially if their supposed power and wealth are inherited or taken through manipulation.

There is nothing wrong with receiving substantial wealth through family or a benevolent benefactor; But the arrival of a truly intelligent being will automatically make the more malevolent power players see that they lack this true superior ability and the grace of someone who uses it with compassion.

We can feel judged by intelligence, what we lack or do not understand will awaken our envy and resentment. Surely it would be a benefit to have a community lifted by a person with this gift. So why does mediocrity thrive in our communities?

To live like this you do not challenge those around you, everyone dumbs down to a level that is subservient and fulfils societal roles to keep the status quo; they keep a supposed peace by diminishing their individuality so that they do not 'stand out in the crowd'. In fact this kind of behaviour is the keystone to envy and jealousy as within the mediocre there are still those who will play a subtle game of manipulative one-upmanship in order to climb the social ladder.

We seek people who bolster our self esteem as much as we seek warmth from a fire. If we encounter those that make us question who we are, they expose the gap between what we are and who we could become.

This is why the exceptional among us stand alone and have suffered by the hands of society (Nikola Tesla is a perfect example). They do this not because they want to, but because they have to in order to protect their intellect. After all, in order to conform and connect to the 'societal hierarchy' they have to fit into that society at a level that is not compatible with their own.

The great philosopher Schopenhauer stated that a uniquely beautiful women also suffers a similar isolation from society. They are instinctively avoided by other women. Being surrounded by true beauty and intellect can (and perhaps should) be the catalyst of change for the mediocre. It could be a time for societal mass psychosis to fall apart so the individuals within can benefit from introspective insights. I am acutely aware that the real madness lies in the herd mentality of our 'evolved' societies. The individuals' intellect and identity has been lost for a very long time.

Intellect will protect itself over ego. Ego will protect itself over progress. I am yet to find a community that places communal intellect over its communal ego. This for me would be a most welcoming place where true expansion and learning would allow for huge growth for all in their psychospiritual expansion.

The battle between ego and intellect is the battle between our ranking position within any group (of two or more souls) as a form of power, over our want to help raise the collective power of said group in an effort to help others grow without prejudice.

As a parent and as a fringe member to every community I have lived in, I have witnessed competitive behaviours that have on occasion given me physical nausea. I have witnessed adults teaching their children within small communities that they must win no matter the cost. I have heard the following; "Us (insert plural of family name).... never lose, beat them like I taught you!" The potential damage for this type of behaviour is immeasurable. It eats away at communities from the inside out. It is a cyclical dis-ease[3] within society that breeds a competitive nature that would rather step on those deemed weak and unworthy. It creates supposed gaps within communities; societal hierarchies that have no actual benefit to the malevolent protagonist or the poor plebeians. This type of behaviour is worthy of a Shakespeare 'Tragedie', although it would be far less intelligible for obvious reasons.

I have so much gratitude for becoming aware of my compassion for others. People continue to mistake my kindness for weakness and I accept this may always be the case. It is much easier to just walk away from toxic

---

[3] 'dis-ease' - The term dis-ease is used by those who choose not to empower health issues by focusing on a particular ailment. The imbalance or disruption of our 'ease', our natural state.

situations believe me. If you rise to the clever antagonist your intelligence will be replaced by emotion and they will sense it, they will love it. Choose where you use your intellect. It is a true gift to be realised and a real sorrow when you give it away to cleverness.

"You can tell whether a man is clever by his answers. You can tell whether a man is wise by his questions." - Naguib Mahfouz.

Fear Not

What is this feeling in my gut,
I've lost my swagger and my strut.
A chill that ripples through my spine,
My hairs on end, a common sign.

Fear has come to steal my thoughts,
I'll let her in and let her talk.
Who am I to question fear?
She's kept me safe throughout the years.

I won't meander from this path,
It's safer here, those woods look dark.
I'll stick to what I'm told is true,
And if you don't then I'll fear you...

Fear, what a fearful word, but not just a word. Words are the expression of energy we feel the need to communicate. The outward expression of the internal processing of our environment, feelings and thoughts. They hold a power that many have forgotten. I have already touched on the fear of intelligence and I have first hand witnessed (with compassion) the ignorance of those that never wish to read, to learn, to expand. It is a choice. We are wisdom seekers you and me. Together we will tackle the deepest and darkest sides of our collective consciousness. To what end? Because exploration is in our DNA and resides within us all. Never give up searching for answers and questioning everything. Never let your fear of the unknown take away your curiosity.

Fear. Say it again… really pronounce it; fear. It has a softness to it It is not plosive, it is more Gaelic than Latin in its phonetics. It makes me want to roll the 'rrrr' at its end to hear it sung in Old Norse by a Valkyrie. It has an 'otherworldly' nature to the word. It is energetic like the word 'fire'.

What do you see in your minds eye when you say it aloud? Where do you feel it in your body. Where does it sit? This is a tool I use to make sense of many words and feelings,. It is also a healing tool for working on suppressed emotions; a tool I use to help clients during therapy and healing sessions.

What is 'Fear' and why do we need it? If you have studied History, Anthropology and Darwinism, they would suggest it is a natural emotion, a response to ones environment. Without fear you would not run from a crocodile, you would take unnecessary risks and your physical genetic line would have disappeared generations ago. I believe the ancient genetics that are within the human bodies we occupy are a mix of many different types of advanced animals and beings, some having mammalian survival instincts and others being more cerebral.

Without going too deep into my exploration of how I believe the human body has developed, I would ask you to please keep an open mind. Some of you may have explored Dolores Cannon's work, I have read about 13 of her transcripts. I would suggest some more grounded esoteric exploration before diving strength into the world of QHHT[4] but you be you.

Once you accept that anything is possible, judgement is replaced by exploration and as a wisdom seeker, for me anything goes. Lets just say I believe that we are more of an experiment than a result of natural evolution (cue book slammed to floor by those not ready, those with 'fear' ;-)). The gaps in evolutionary biology still do not explain the huge leap from the many varieties of Homo - habilis, erectus, rudolfensis, heidelbergensis, floriensis, neanderthalensis, naledi, and luzonensis; to the solitary Homo sapiens that inhabits the world today. If you were to create a conscious intelligent avatar (physical body) on a dangerous but bountiful planet (Earth before humanity), the most important criteria would be:

Consciousness - You would want an individual in this species to be aware of it's sensations, perceptions, ideas, feelings and attitudes in a lateral path.

---

[4] Dolores Canon's Quantum Healing Hypnotherapy Technique.

Adaptability - To be able to react to changes to ones environment in order to thrive not just to survive.

Dexterity - To be able to manipulate the natural environment in order to create, change or destroy objects, make tools to build, hunt, cook etc.

Intelligence - At the core and linked to all of the above. You would want this being to be at the very top of the food chain when it comes to intelligence. Having a brain big enough in comparison to its body size so that its complexity is far and above all other species in its environment.

Nobody truly knows how other animals think or feel. I do not believe we truly understand other humans either but we have the same base materials and it would be reasonable to suggest we are all relatively similar. A Crow has feelings, shows signs of intelligence, adaptability, dexterity and consciousness. It could not outcompete a human and unfortunately they are hunted by farmers who fear the damage they can cause to young livestock (no real evidence for this but hey ho). But the crow is not a human. We have a unique skill, something that I believe only a few other mammals have on this planet. We 'manifest'.

I do not think this needs too much explanation, other than to say we not only try and manifest abundance and happiness but we unconsciously manifest fear as well. We are so good at this it has become an instinctive, subconscious power that is out of many humans' control. The fear and turmoil manifested by most of humanity is ironically what I 'fear' the most. It keeps many of us aware beings from wanting to be in the company of the 'chaotic' for too long. It is exhausting to be surrounded by unstable emotions; the fear and anger of other beings who have no idea just how powerful they are.

I had an encounter recently. A person was trying to recruit me into a social group that was at its core aimed at destroying a person whom they believed had caused a lot of suffering to them. Nothing to do with me. As an INFJ Sigma[5] (the closest match I have ever found to

_____

[5] INFJ and 'Sigma' explained in the chapter 'Sigma Stigma'.

explain how I think, feel and act), all I could feel and see were red flags. For confirmation (never truly needed at this point of my journey), they then proceeded to ask me if I knew how to curse people. 'Hand slapping front of my face emoji', I was honest, saying 'yes I do, and no I won't and I don't'.

They were using the threat of a (vaguely) potential attack on me to strengthen the aggressive fear of a group against one human who was driven by their own fear into causing these social issues in the first place.

I do not like some of the terms the 'awake' use against those who are unaware: zombies, muggles, sleep-walkers, NPC's[6] etc. But I knew pretty much exactly what they were going to say and why before they had even arrived. This is a superpower and one that every human has the potential to use. Would it be safe for every single human on Earth to have this level of intuitive and cognitive ability?… NO. Lets call the ones who are definitely not ready (unless real hell is to be unleashed), the 'unconscious'.

---

[6] NPC - Non Player Character from role-playing games such as Red Dead Redemption where the characters are seemingly alive but are computer generated or programmed.

I always think about the theory of the Van Allen belt. The beautiful theory that may be scary to the unconscious but I find resonates very deeply and makes a lot of sense.

The scientific explanation: The Van Allen belts consists of two doughnut shaped belts of charged particles (protons and electrons), trapped by the Earths magnetic field and orbiting our planet. They are nicknamed the 'radiation' belts and said to be a natural phenomena.

The psychospiritual theory: Some theorise that we cannot pass through the belts and we never have (cue fake moon landing conspiracies). They claim that they shield our power of manifestation from the rest of the universe. That our galaxy and the universe in its infinite size are directly affected by the uncontrolled fear and unconscious manifestations of humanity on Earth (at our current awareness). It goes deeper still... Some also believe that this belt and our evolution are controlled by a very large space station full of advanced technology in a fixed orbit around our Earth. An orbit that mimics the Earths orbit of the Sun. An orbit that has one side fixed in place due to tidal locking. This 'dusty Death Star' (I claim this quote!) Is our Moon.

I have used this example many many times to gauge whether I can have an open-minded conversation with someone without prejudice. It turns out that even spiritual folk get a little bit triggered when you tell them 'Grandmother Moon' may be an old broken down starship; a remnant of a cold war in space between advanced civilisations of higher beings. I should not find it fun to trigger people but I honestly cannot help it. It is a natural reaction to honesty. You see I fear the actions of unconscious minds around my children at school, the reactivity of the unconscious around my wife when I am not there to protect her. Small triggers can instigate big changes, call it planting seeds, I see it more like ploughing the fields to unearth what lies beneath (often the land is barren).

Now you may be seeing some patterns emerging that are coming together. I hope you are seeing why I have spent so much time writing this book. Society, our buried shadows, the system, healing, fear, consciousness and magik are all deeply connected. If we understand them deeply and work with them daily we become far more powerful and potentially dangerous to any form of control. We become an object of fear, we become the monster or demon that so many people are brain-washed into fearing. We become whole again. This is my path, as a couple my wife and I affectionately call it the path of the 'Mystical Warrior'. It is a bit cheesy but it is light and helps us to not take everything too seriously. We often joke that if one of us came home from a drive and said they had just been abducted by Aliens the other would simply say - 'Oh how cool is that! What did they say?'.

I suppose my point is (there are way too many to put into one book) I am truly fearful of a mass awakening. So many spiritual types are so keen for this conscious awakening of souls to their true potential. I think a nice steady natural approach is probably what nature or the Gods, Source etc. intends for us. It should come slowly with books like this and through one to one discussions. Small and steady steps, not in the 'right' direction but in any direction that our free minds wish to take us.

My own spiritual awakening journey in this life has been incredibly painful and isolating, it is by far the hardest path. It is slow and painful and often so frightening I have often been consumed by fear and had to purposefully block my chakras in order to stop progress for some time.

People talk about 'The Great Solar Flash'. The energy increase preparing us for the Sun's inevitable changing of the consciousness of this planet. The scientifically explainable increase in solar activity is theorised to be due to an increase in energy fired at us from the Sun (the conscious being).

This is said to be a cyclical pattern that happens when civilisations reach a peek in technology and a trough in consciousness. Imagine humans as AI rather than conscious natural souls. Think Atlantis and its inevitable destruction due to the abominations it created through cloning, greed, manipulation and unbalanced power. Our Sun is our horse so to speak. We are passenger on a space rock (Earth) that is a rider of this 'horse' which is on its own journey around the Milky Way. The Milky

Way is on its own journey through the universe and so on. Yet we still fight for toilet paper in a man-made, capitalist driven, potentially made-up crisis. We still ostracise someone for being different. We still give our children to state education and watch with joy as their imagination is smothered and their connection to source is lacerated.

I know we are eternal spiritual beings living a human existence, I think that this existence is crucial to a developing soul and therefore the experience is protected by even higher beings. If there is too much of an imbalance in consciousness amongst a race such as ours, it would make sense that a great reset would occur. Otherwise what would be the point in living? Lessons need to be learnt that I am sure of; but if a malevolent minority of power hungry beings who thrive on the oppression of consciousness and gain power from shepherding humanity are creating too much of an imbalance… it may be time for a mass awakening. Fear and anger make us malleable and weak. We look outside of ourselves for comfort, we rely on our governments and societal ideals even if we know that they are lying to us and using us.

"A ship in harbour is safe, but that's not what ships are built for." - William Shedd.

Be honest with yourselves: Would you rather take the 'blue pill' and remain in a state of blissful ignorance and the illusion of ordinary reality; or take the red pill, accept a painful reality and go on the deep dive of becoming aware of unsettling truths.

Once you take the red pill (so to speak) there is no going back. You start to see patterns all around you (in the Matrix movie they called it code). Behaviours and actions, emotions and propaganda become obvious and comical. Once the dust has settled you notice that everything about you has changed, the way you see yourself, your life and others around you.

If you are relatively new to this open-minded idea of self-expansion through exploration of ideas and theory; this chapter itself has been laced with 'fear traps' to probe your ideologies. I have touched on some very fringe subjects and given no real evidence or explanation, just theory. I have purposefully gone deeper into the esoteric to see if it triggers you. I will never know if this is the case but you the reader know.

At which points in this article did you really want to have your say, make reactive social media response full of emoji's, or just put the book down? I hope at least once. This means you have work to do. If you do not live with fear it would not matter if the words in this book do not align with your worldly construct.

I get triggered all the time. I will forever be learning why this is the case. More importantly I consciously practice how to not let the resulting emotions consume me and take control of my intellect; resulting in a reaction that I will most probably regret. Fear takes away your power until it takes control of your actions. You no longer act as a conscious being, you are driven by a negative emotional intelligence and become the unconscious observer. Let us replace our fear of the unknown with childlike curiosity. Let us all wake up as individuals, master our fears, become conscious again and unite in this awakened freedom.

"Courage is resistance to fear, mastery of fear, not absence of fear." - Mark Twain

We Are All Connected

You feel their joy, sorrow, their energy,
Not just through words, but some kind of synergy.
It becomes a challenge to hold back your tears,
When they talk of their childhood and difficult years.

You muster the courage to actively listen,
To hold space; to bear witness, their healthy transition.
The connection you feel can be felt with the all,
No stranger of awareness and also the fool.

All that exists have feelings, are one,
We embrace the illusion that we are alone.
Alone we struggle but through suffering we learn,
This life is for living our connections are earnt.

Finally the science seems to be catching up with what was has been known as the pseudoscience-fiction.

There is a biological, chemical and atomic connection between everything that exists in physical reality. So says Neil deGrasse Tyson the spiritual cynic with a great scientific mind. For those of us that journey into the unseen realms and have working relationships with all kinds of higher beings and the universe itself… we feel there is still hope for humanity and its expansion beyond just the science.

Now that scientists are starting to theorise the existence of alternate realities and dimensions, it is becoming more acceptable for us wisdom seekers to have open discussions about Source connection and interconnectivity.

As Carl Sagan once said; "we are a way for the cosmos to know itself". We are the biological machines that give consciousness a voice to experience itself in a unique and individual way that is still truly connected to all that there is. How does this connection work? Why can we not all feel it all the time?

These are the wrong questions, they are the obvious ones. You have to think and feel about it subjectively. You have to experience your connectivity in your own way because your experience is unique. We share our experiences in the physical realm, we share a dinner with family, a movie with friends or a bottle of wine. The key is realising our 'relationships' with the people, the places, the Earth, everything that surrounds and is within us. They are all that there is. "Everything in the universe only exists because it is in relationship to everything else. Nothing exists in isolation" - Margaret J. Wheatley.

The deeper you study your physical and spiritual relationships, the closer you will come to understanding what they mean to you. Relationships take time. You have to build trust, show respect for yourself and it/they/them; witness a slow and steady understanding with everything you connect with. On a quantum level we are all connected regardless of space and time. From a human perspective, space and time are relative to our relationships and connections, certainly in the physical realm, our Earth dream. For many of us, it is the conversation we have, our close relationships, a good or bad feeling we get when we meet somebody for the first time. It is the feeling we get when we witness the sunrise or a clear starry night for the first time in months.

We are all so incredibly busy and this busyness is unique to the individual. Healthy times of procrastination look different now than they did in the 1980's when I was a child. Life was simpler without mobiles and super computers. Sure, I had a console and would spend hours on my own in my room in my pre and early teens, perfecting Super Mario Kart. But I also journaled an awful lot. From at least 11 years old I would write prose and music to help make sense of my thoughts and feelings about the world around me. On a regular visit to my Mother in my early thirties she handed me a few large files filled with at least a thousand poems, songs and doodles from my earlier years. I wish I knew where these were, unfortunately I think they have been burnt by my Father in a clearing clutter phase, along with other precious artefacts from my childhood.

Thankfully I still have my memory. I can still remember how I felt when I sat alone deeply connected to a source of universal intelligence, a consciousness that was as overwhelming as it was exciting. It was this 'deepness' that I was criticised for as a child. It is this 'deepness' that I search for signs of in humanity. It is the small talk that exhausts me. The shallow interactions that drain my energy. I hope my words reach some of you and bring back memories of your early years where you explored connections in isolation. I hope you know that me and you are connected, we have something in common… we exist and we are aware of this existence.

I wrote this short story after having a vivid recall of a moment in my teens.

During a meditation I asked for moral guidance on the cutting of energetic ties with close family members, it was a particularly tough time of letting go and moving on. I believe my guides were trying to show me the bigger picture. Ever cryptic, the message was not clear at first. A few years later and it is starting to sink in…

We Are All Connected…

This hangover had a energetic buzz to it. For some reason I can still not explain I felt on top of the world. No matter the amount of poison I had consumed the night before everything felt 'floaty', sublime and melancholy at the same time, it felt beautiful and somewhat intensely so.

I was in London on a tube (subway) on a Sunday morning heading towards Paddington Station. Everyone was doing the usual heads down, eyes focussed on their laps or a book, headphones firmly on or just minding their own business; as is the 'correct' etiquette on the Underground. Everyone apart from us.

She was sat opposite me but maybe a few seats to my right side. I watched her as she observed her surroundings with a calmness and grace that had me mesmerised. She was too beautiful. Mousey coloured thick hair with the hint of a curl, dark brown eyes with a hint of gold. I felt like I knew her, like we had caught the same carriage together but couldn't get seats next to each other; we were just taking in our surroundings.

I was looking straight into her eyes transfixed on this angelic being, every inch of my body was vibrating. I felt something, not love, not lust, not anything I can describe in words other than a true, tangible connection. She felt safe and warm and honest and natural, she felt like home. We felt connected. More than that, we felt bonded, more than lovers or family, almost as if we were fragments of the same soul that had been re-united after a thousand lives apart.

Time had quite literally stopped, we were not on the tube, we were flying through space, we were the stars the planets, the galaxies and all the space in between.

A jolt in the carriage brought us both back to earth as we were reacquainted with our egos and suddenly realised we were both engaged in a mutual stare.

I instantly looked away, embarrassed for some reason about my slightly disheveled appearance to a complete stranger. But she was no stranger, I could feel her gaze float back onto me from time to time as I pretended to read the tube map above the windows of the carriage, anything to keep my eyes from being pulled back into hers.

Who is she? Why do I feel like this? Why did I suddenly feel so exposed and vulnerable, so alone? I wanted so badly to look at her or to say 'Hi'. I wanted so badly to reclaim my confidence that she had taken from me. A minute before we were floating through the cosmos together in divine connection, I had felt her love and compassion, her knowing, I had quite literally felt like I was her and she was me. I had now devolved back into a seventeen year old boy. The truth is that she had given me much much more than I could understand at that time. My teenage mind had taken the reins. 'Does she fancy me? She is sooooo fit. I've got to get her number. How do I ask for it? What just happened? God I smell like booze. How's my hair looking? How long until Paddington Station? I've got to do something quick.'

Time had been reawakened again and as it is always does, it ran it's course...

The doors of the carriage opened and I clumsily left the train, head down with my eyes to the floor. With my two feet firmly on the platform I turned around as the doors to her carriage closed. Our eyes met through the glass and she gave me one more gift, she smiled. I felt a knowing feeling, a remembering. We *had* known each other and this *was* a reunion. In some way in some capacity we would meet again. But not as people; this was a deeper connection. We had both recognised each other whilst being in a higher state of consciousness observing the 3D world around us. The connection was tangible, I felt it in every inch of my body and deeper still. The only other time I have felt this connection to another human on this level in this life is with my wife. I am incredibly fortunate to be blessed with such a gift and believe me it was a long and learning journey before

I met her when I was in my mid-thirties; this time I did not let the doors close on our carriage.

I sometimes think back to my 'angel on the tube'. I thank her for teaching me what a real connection is. I thank her for helping me to remember so that when it happened again (and it did) I would recognise it and never let it go. No words were ever passed between us, only a handful of minutes, a short and innocent stare and what could have been perceived as a romantic smile between two teenagers. She may have left me in body but I will never forget her spirit. We were forged from the same iron, from the same star dust. She is in me and my wife, my children and their lives. She is a connection to all that may feel impossible to find until you stop and observe.

She is the connection that we try to ignore but someday come to realise may have shaped this life.

"My best relationship is the one I have with myself. I know I am always connected to a Universe that loves me. I draw loving people and loving experiences to me"
- Louise Hay.

Why A Shaman?

The troubled young man lies still in the bed,
While doctors and nurses probe in his head.
He watches, aware that they think he is sleeping,
They see his eyes open but doubt on his thinking.

He sees the connection; this moment and all,
He's playing the part of observer and fool.
There's nothing to do but feed him with pills,
They'll numb and they'll blind him from lessons yet still...

He'll carry on living and learning and loving,
Till one day he'll break from these chains and keep moving.
To far away places and other realms,
He'll find solace in leaving them all here in Hell.

Yes, I can feel you thinking it. How very dark!!!

I wrote that poem when I was 15 years old. My English teacher had lost my GCSE English Literature coursework and this being before the use of computers for such things, I had a week to re-write some creative literature or have my overall grade drop considerably. I cannot explain how I seemed to have a vision of my future. It would be almost a decade later that I would start to have severe periods of anguish, mentally and spiritually. These were my Shamanic initiations and until I would formally heed the call, they did not go away...

After my first significant psychosis at the ripe age of 23, the world that had been carefully constructed to support me fell apart. Blessed and cursed with a private education and an empaths disposition; I had been trained to think through problems and my natural 'deep feels' had been smothered and extinguished by a military education. I had pushed my most powerful gift so deep that for many of my formative years I stumbled through life relying on an intellect that had not blossomed; all the time a fierce fire was brewing just beneath the surface. The facade was starting to crack.

Without full disclosure, I did not work for any Secret Service or clandestine group although I may have had opportunities to do so. I did sign non-disclosure agreements and I will honour them for my own sake even though I was not actually privy to any information of any significance or interest.

The short version of the story… I totally lost my mind whilst working as a sub-contractor for the government. It didn't take very long, it's all a bit of a blur but maybe it was 6 months, maybe a bit longer. I witnessed behaviours, programs and a sickness within the system that I could not ignore. It was unlike anything I could have imagined and I started to lose sleep (maybe one day I will be honest about what really happened to me in those dark days, the results of which took me down a cyclical path of searching, observing, evaluating and losing my mind). Two weeks of no sleep and continuous physical and mental stress has an interesting effect on the body and mind. Fat is quickly stripped from your body, your brain needs to eat and it turns out I wasn't sitting still enough to actually see the significance of any sustenance.

I was arrested whilst making a 'citizens arrest' outside of a government building. I had been pushed so far that everyone had become a threat. The police quickly realised that the issue was with me and not the poor man I held firmly to the ground. There is paranoia and then there is deep and dark psychosis. As my thinking mind gave way, something far stronger was released. I look back and wonder how I could still walk in a straight line, let alone drive to work, small talk my way to my desk and check my e-mails. My intuitive energy and connection to the universe had resurfaced. All of my pain and childhood suffering that had been buried deep, everything had resurfaced. Now it was time for a short break. A minimum of 28 days in an institute. My freedoms removed as I was told I was a potential threat to myself and others. Faced with a lot of time to try and make sense of what had just happened, I found myself praying for help and guidance. I was never a true believer of the Bible or religion, but in those dark days I found comfort and strength in prayer to Jesus. The warmth and peace was so tangible that I knew I had to search, observe and evaluate this. I needed answers and yearned for purpose.

18 years later, I have dived into and out of Buddhism, various martial arts, Yoga and Wicca. All inspiring and insightful but none resonated with my soul as much as the world's indigenous practices of Shamanism...

What is it? I still find it fascinating that although the whole world practiced it in some form or other with huge and unmistakeable similarities; it has mostly been forgotten.

In one sentence: A healer who enters altered states of consciousness in order to interact with the spirit world. But so so much more than that...

The word "Shaman" comes from the Tungusic word samān, which may have originated from the Evenki or Manchu language. It originates from Eastern and

Central Siberia and is the word used by visiting Russians who interacted with indigenous peoples of Siberia. The word translates to 'the one who sees', as the Russians believed that these healers could quite literally see spirits and other realms.

The word that originated from the Evenki people (of Mongolia) has now evolved to describe anyone who practices a similar form of spiritual healing. Many call this cultural appropriation; I feel that it is more innocent than this. Certainly for the Neo-Shamanic or core practitioners of the Western World. It has become a metonymic phrase that encompasses a broad range of spiritual practices. I have come across 'Shamanic Practitioners' within the United Kingdom that are clearly focussed on Druidism or Wicca but offer certain healing tools that are indistinguishable from say the practice of a typically Shamanic 'Soul Retrieval'.

A Shaman is far more than just a mid-life crisis (trigger alert) who does a weekend workshop and believes they are ready to heal people. I do not wish to be critical but if I have learnt anything at all about my spiritual practice… it cannot be done over a 'zoom' call. It can only be done in a 'sacred space' when a client is with you in person. This is not not a universal healing modality. It is a calling. A calling that usually comes from a place of deep darkness and suffering. It is not a quick fix for the healer or the client and is a practice not a perfection. A channelling of energy for the betterment of land and community.

I will re-iterate a quote I have found on a forum doing research. Such a treasure to find wisdom amongst so much misleading information. It is a shame I cannot quote the author (I am working on this) but this is to me, what the noun 'Shaman' should or could mean.

'A Shaman may use magical means to act, but a Shaman is a cultural role not a magical title. They are the culturally sanctioned outside perspective, the one who can see beyond the structures of the society and so help the people to live together in spite of and within their culture. The Shaman is a mediator: Between the self and the other, the people and the world, the seen and the unseen. They act to dissolve boundaries and do so safely, helping to guide others in their development within their roles. The Shaman can freely reflect whatever is needed for the person who seeks their help, and shift between many personas and roles that may or may not exist within their society. They heal, and they teach, and they question, and they manipulate for the good of the people, with the consent of those in their tribe. Most Shamans use some kind of entheogenic substance or practice to help their activities, and all Shaman's alter their state of consciousness to access alternate ideas and points of view.' - Anon.

On paper Shamanism looks like a selfless and beautiful community driven spiritual practice, so why has it been forgotten by so many of us?

I have been down this rabbit hole for years. There is so much confirmation bias within the information available so I will do my best to 'sit on the fence'. I have compassion for all of humanity but not for all religious practices. The fact remains that there is no empirical evidence for Shamanic practice within the Celtic tribes. There is however an abundance of evidence for trance state healing, herbalism, magik (not rabbit-out-of-hat 'magic'), Animism and most significantly, seasonal and daily rituals revolving around nature.

I have spent a lot of time reading actual literature and browsing for answers; please do your own research because much of what I have learnt has the potential to upset stout Christians and many other religious practices that have removed 'Nature' from their worship (or arguably risen above Nature) to worship an unseen, inaccessible, off-world monotheistic deity. I would suggest research or learning how to do a 'journey' to find and build relationships with spirits and guides that will help you to remember who and what you are.

Perhaps we should find new nouns to describe our practices? While it is bonding to bring a community of healers together under the same terms, we are all uniquely different and practice our healings subjectively. Many healers I have met have other jobs, other roles in society. When I ask them what they do for a living they find it difficult to give a clear answer. Perhaps they do not want to be bound to one role just for the sake of conversation and polite nosiness! Small talk, it is our kryptonite.

My mentors (I have been beyond fortunate to have some great ones), without necessarily knowing each other have had one thing in common; whilst under their care, in their protective training 'bubble', the work is done exactly as they teach it. Until this work is practiced proficiently by the student there is no deviation whatsoever… Once they are happy that the wisdom has been passed on safely, in all cases they have said 'go out and heal and see how your healing methods change to become your own'. There is a lineage of course, but it seems to be flexible. Within months of using a new healing tool they do not look, feel or sound exactly the same as the method taught under their watchful eyes. You could argue that as a Western Practitioner I am being trained from a soup of knowledge taken from cultures all over the world. This would be correct. Years of research have led me to believe that Shamanic principles of the Celtic world have been hidden so well by religious dogma that you are better off researching

Druidism, Wicca or Herbalism to get an idea of how our ancestors would have put their wisdom into practice.

Are you a 'Shaman' or a 'Shamanic Practitioner'? Are you a 'Spiritual Healer' or simply an 'Energy Worker/ Mover'? We have normalised appropriation in our culture and forgotten how our ancestors practice. If I had to answer honestly: I am an Animystic who can heal and is fluid in my practice. I rather like saying I study 'Animysticism' but I think that may be something to do with my ego and not yet a registered word.

It is time to move on, dig deep and reawaken. Let us stop punishing ourselves for the past and start working for our future.

Whatever you are and whatever you practice, keep up the good work. It is your intention behind your actions that is most important whether it upsets people or not. On our website www.badcallbayretreat.com my wife and I call ourselves 'Shamanic Practitioners', it is a common term that is becoming acceptable to use within our society; trust is being regained after so many years of suppression and many people are beginning to 'see' that spiritual practices do not have to be tribalistic and rigid. They can be fluid and subjective and so can we all.

My dream is that one day there will be so many healers on this planet that the saturation tips the balance and allows for a spiritual and psychological evolution for humanity that is well overdue...

My fear is that the hidden puppeteers of our societies, the clandestine businesses and secret handshakers of the world do not want us to re-ignite these powerful ancient practices. They want us to rely on our minds, our minds that have been cleverly disconnected from our souls through processed food, chemicals, 9 to 5 jobs that disregard the seasons and our need for hibernation; the crucial behavioural adaptation that is a natural call to reconnect to nature and to our higher selves. It has been silenced with cortisone inducing social media, virtual reality, artificial intelligence and World Wars. All in the name of the evolution of our species with the resulting devolution of the individual.

Humanity thrives on working out a challenge. I used to call myself a 'problem solving mechanical engineer' now I just call myself a wisdom seeker but I'm not finding a lot of wisdom out there if I am honest.

We do not want this world they are promising. We do not want a world without challenges, it sounds like a dystopian nightmare. Just the same, we do not want to live as perfectly behaving angelic beings, that is not living. Living is about growth, it is not about a final destination it is about the journey and how you deal with the final destination... death. If we become the Orwellian nightmare that he[7] predicted there will be no room for spiritual growth

There is no growth in times of peace, there is no true evolution for the individual or the species. Peace is a part of repetitive cycle, some believe it is a 100-year cycle and that periods of war and peace are inevitable and necessary.

---

[7] George Orwell 1903-1950. Famous for dystopian works of fiction including: 'Animal Farm', 'Ninteen Eighty-Four' and 'Down and Out in Paris and London'.

Thankfully, perfection and heaven are religious concepts, for true perfection comes in the form of a misshaped carrot, heavy rain through beams of sunlight, the hug and intimacy after a falling out with my wife or when my kids tell me without prompting that they love me. Those moments, witnessed and cherished, they are why I still fight, and love.

I have met many people who do not believe in spirituality. I think this is akin to saying you do not believe in art.

Everything is a spiritual experience; waking up, having breakfast, watching the sun rise and fall, everything we do and observe has purpose and meaning. There is a consciousness to all and our feelings are included.

Please find your connection. Mine is a path of seeking wisdom so that I can forever be fluid of thought and never arrive at an ultimate answer. Please whatever you do, do not let your physical age guide your ego into believing it is wise.

"True wisdom is gained by understanding that you don't know everything. True ignorance is established when you believe you do." - Michael Gallien.

Sigma Stigma

How Society Misunderstands and Judges Sigma Empaths and Intuitive Introverts (INFJ's)

The ones to look out for but not to fear,
The stranger who rescues you from your tears.
She's gone in a flash no need for reward,
She's too busy watching the living chessboard.

Do not run after her, get on with your day,
If you have nothing to tell her then be on your way.
She's quiet and humble unless you provoke her,
Don't challenge a lioness, don't try and choke her.

She's invisible until she finds an imbalance,
You can't hide your evil from her upcoming challenge.
You'll be left exposed and you won't know why,
Your tormented followers will shudder and cry.

"How deep, how scary, how weird, how bizarre"
She doesn't mind slander and that sets her apart.
She's the watcher of keepers that run this old zoo,
Before you have noticed her, she'll know you.

It is a very human thing to try and see where we fit into sliding scales. We have an obsession with naming everything we see around us and categorising it. We do this with all the flora and fauna on Earth and all the stars and yet unexplained phenomena beyond our Galaxy. It is comfortable for our egos to feel that we know how we fit in the society around us, it makes us feel comfortable to fit into the theatre of society. Once we think we know where we belong we play this role with vigour and if we are not careful we will defend this role with our lives even if we have an opportunity to grow and change.

True defiance is more than just a gesture it is a way of life. I am not interested in fitting in or conforming to societal expectations. I often say to people 'I am not here to make friends, that should happen naturally if I am a good person and welcomed'. If it does not happen naturally then the people I am around are not worth my energy. They will still get my compassion but I will not lie to them and align with their ideals if they do not fit my own. Societal norms are a dress code for a party I will not attend. I do not just ignore the rules, by exposing them I strip them of all the power they try and hold on to.

Being a non conformist is not being an anarchist. I do not walk around trying to change everything that does to fit with my ideals. Although I have found that this often happens naturally through the consistency of my mood and morals. These are all capable of change, I do not walk around with a permanent smile on my face, I have a variable moral compass depending on a situation. If I am attacked I will have compassion and a perhaps a defensive stance against the attacker. If my children are attacked then I became a different animal altogether. It is a natural defence for innocence and the innocent that drives me to make changes in my life and my immediate environment. If I feel that those under my care are not safe I will change their environment, not to stop them from learning valuable life lessons (an amount of suffering is essential for us all to grow), but to make it acceptable to keep them physically and spiritually in a space where they can learn without real danger of sudden uncontrollable threat. This is not easy in a world that is overflowing with minds that have a tendency to 'react' without an able response (response-ability). If we were all truly responsible for our actions or inactions then our children would be able to grow in an environment where only the chaos of nature would be their primary threat, She would be a tool for their personal growth without the need of 'helicopter parenting' I try so hard not to enact.

I am not a fan of typecasting and I truly believe that our personalties change throughout our lives and sometimes throughout a day depending on changes to our exterior environment. The 'you' that goes to work and functions within a peaceful societal construct is not the 'you' that would survive during a time of war where you are responsible for the survival of the innocent members of your family and community. Nevertheless I find it interesting that there is an abundance of information available for personality traits, not the 'take a quiz and see who you are' nonsense but the psychological papers and books that are available to all if you are interested. Youtube does a good job for those who have a short attention span or feel they do not have enough time to read. As always be aware of 'click-bait', and also be aware that you think you have no time to read actual literature but you probably spend an hour or two a day watching absolute nonsense on the internet...

Socionics divides people into 16 different types, called sociotypes some of which are; ESTJ, ENTJ, ISTJ, INTJ, INFJ etc. A formal conversion is carried out following the Myers–Briggs Type Indicator. The MBTI claims to categorise individuals into tho psychological and personality types. I am exhausted just typing them out! Please lose yourself in these acronyms if this resonates with you. The internet is all yours! I am not a fan of acronyms but at least these 16 types give a wider variety to box your personality within. We have become accustomed to the Alpha, Beta, Omega, Gamma, Delta system. After taking both tests I have been informed I am a Sigma INFJ.

My intuition tells me that the type of people that will be drawn to read this book will have very similar personality traits to the Sigma INFJ.

Sigma - 'denoting a high-achieving individual who pursues his or her own goals rather than being part of a social hierarchy'. Collins Dictionary

INFJ - Stands for "introverted, intuitive, feeling and judging". People with this personality type are also known as "the Advocate" or "the Idealist".

We will just call the Sigma INFJ the 'Sigmas' for the sake of this chapter.

They are independent people who rarely depend on others. They refuse to sacrifice their peace for someone else's approval, so they will often prefer solitude over needy small talk. They are strong and silent, often called the 'lone wolves' of society. They focus on living a life that feels right to them. For them, real strength lies in being comfortable with who you trust and who you are.

Sigmas do not get affected by social hierarchies. They understand people and how they fit in to their personalities and societal roles. They do not need this social structure to survive and others may see this as arrogance and aloofness.

Following their own compass works better than following the crowd. They are often confused with being a more withdrawn version of an Alpha male. Alpha males, draw attention and showcase themselves. A Sigma is quietly confident, they will be listened too and people will play less games with them but rather seek their opinion. Alpha males carefully craft there image to showcase their power. They are performers, flexing achievements and staging power moves. They thrive on being noticed for their success and seniority.

A Sigma lives in the moment, is more natural and his simple presence and authenticity will earn him respect without any grandiose behaviours. Alphas struggle to challenge Sigmas as they do not put on a show. They will either stand up to an Alpha or just walk away, they can choose to be the Alpha or not depending on whether they see it is necessary.

Sigmas make up only 0.02% of the global populace. They are incredibly rare and you will know if you meet or are one. They stand out, even if they would rather be in the shadows.

The Sigma is not an anarchist but will weigh social expectations against his own principles and peace of mind. He knows that the real challenge lies in living with big decisions, but they do not measure themselves on others and find strength in a healthy self-assurance. These are the rare people that enjoy work, from mundane to highly complicated tasks. They will not moan about the weather or gossip about the school mums. They realise that their choices preserve the peace and integrity that they value so highly.

If you are quiet and reserved within your community it will not take long for people to start filling in the gaps themselves. Before long they will create an idealised version of you. Through gossip and their own individual observations they will come together to form this 'you' that is most probably not who you are. Over time and if you feel it is necessary; you may decide to let parts of your 'self' to be known. As you are in constant change and on a wisdom journey, this version of you will not remain the same.

Society does not think for itself it is its own body and it is frightened of what does not conform or fit within its structure. I see society as a living breathing entity. I see the people within it playing there everyday roles and conforming to a rigid structure that they seem oblivious to.

People ask for honesty but actually they are scared of it. Most people are not ready for this level of honesty. A Sigma will give you nothing but honesty. They notice you making mistakes and find it difficult to keep quiet if being honest may help your progress. People get upset or offensive when they are given uncomfortable truths over comfortable lies.

The Sigma does not help for gain but they will expect you to listen to them if they have listened to you. If you have pets you will find they are very likely to focus their attention on them rather tham you. This is not to appease you and get in your favour, they genuinely prefer the company of animals and non-judgmental beings. They understand and enjoy the company of nature, nature beings and higher beings. It is the middle ground beings, the human beings (the dangerous ones) that they study, observe and often need space from.

When they need to recharge there abundant energy, they will quietly slip away from the party or society and not be seen until they feel replenished. When Sigmas reach the tipping point of loss of energy for gain of knowledge, they will disappear. What is so different about them is how they recharge. Most will take recreative drugs, lay on a sun lounger and try and do nothing. The Sigma will take this time to process all that he has recently learnt. They will analyse all the data like scientists and fit it all into the algorithm they have spent their whole lives constructing. For them, this is recharging the batteries and getting ready for more data.

Small talk… they cannot do it. It is the epitome of societal nonsense. They do not think they are better than you but they need deep conversations to gain deeper insights. They will accept a conversation about the meaning of life with a complete stranger. This will not be 'too deep' a conversation it will excite them and they will appreciate it.

People will not understand them and so they will not fully express what they know of themselves or a situation. They are aware that they will forever be on a journey of self-exploration and evolution so it may seem redundant to express who they are if they are always changing. They are also aware that as they will never conform to a specific role within community or society, people will always be slightly uncomfortable in their presence. They are complicated and they do not try to make themselves more accessible by dumbing down who they are in order for people to accept them. They have learnt from experience that if they truly open up and give people a brief glimpse of their mind and their intuitive perspective, it will often make people uncomfortable; it may trigger them and make them question themselves for a brief moment... long enough to know that they would rather live in ignorance. 'Where ignorance is bliss, 'tis folly to be wise' Thomas Gray. An intuitive will know that some people are better off not knowing what lies ahead or what is right in front of them. Ignorance is not stupidity. I see it as a defence mechanism for those who are either not ready to work on themselves or those who have tried to gain insight and have decided that encumbering their minds with worry was too painful; that they would rather just not know.

In conclusion, I think I reject the script altogether. I feel I have a relatively defined sense of self and it just seems to be more adaptable and changeable than one simple trait. If I need to be an Alpha then I am, if I need to step back from a situation and let someone else take control then so be it. It makes no odds to me either way, I will observe a situation and be whatever I need to be depending on the environment I find myself in. I suppose that is why although given many opportunities to become a soldier, I rejected them based on the knowledge that I would feel uncomfortable in a fixed role as a commanding officer. I did not like the idea that I would potentially lead men and women into battle with the full awareness that they may be more capable of keeping my unit alive. The postcode or life lottery does not (for me) give people the right to bark orders at others. Should my genetics and schooling be any different?

I am not easily distracted by money and societal roles. We were not a wealthy family. My Mother and Father were from typical 'working class' backgrounds although their natural intelligence, ambition and work ethics were well above average. I am privileged (through bursaries) to have a private education. I have also experienced the UK state schooling system. As parents we have chosen home-education over its 'iron claw'.

At 15 years of age whilst studying at a military school in the South of England, we were all subjected to a government skill assessment test, a consensus test to let us know what kind of job we were heading for after schooling. None of us took this seriously. I personally had an idea of my worth before the test and the results just helped me to realise (even at that relatively young age) that the system was a total farce and a suppressor of our youths'. It seems that even though my parents were paying an extortionate amount of money for my education (with a 60% bursary), we were still subjected to the total nonsensical subjugation of the system.

I was offered the opportunity of being a bin man after my private education was finished. Obviously my aptitude and intelligence quotation was a good fit for this role in society. I think this is an admirable and necessary job but I had a different vision for myself. I have since met many bin men that love their jobs and the benefits that are bestowed upon them include sick pay, holiday pay and a surprisingly good salary. Early starts mean early finishes and I have met a few that appreciated that the time they could spend with their families. Their working day would start at the crack of dawn but finish in the early afternoon.

There should be no judgement for the jobs and roles we have. The only true judge is ourselves. If you are grounded in reality and confront your own shadows you will live in integrity regardless of what you do to pay for your bills.

This chapter is self-centred. I suppose I am what they call a Sigma INFJ, although I feel we are all much more complex than any personality 'type'. If it helps, I have spent most of my life engaged in self-flagellation. I was silent until my teens and now I have found my voice. It has been very difficult finding the confidence to write this book. I have had to seek a self worth that has not been embedded by family and friends. I have had to figure it all out for myself, by myself and figure out who my 'self' is. Nonetheless, no one (except my wife) has ever even scratched the surface of understanding the core of who I am. There is a small amount of peace in knowing that I am not alone. That there are other 'weirdos' out there. I live with one and I have met a few. They are the ones that you get lost in deep conversation with on your first meet. You feel like your time with them is on a clock and they are so interesting that you wish they would stay. They are rare and crucial. They think so far outside of the box that they would be a threat to most people if they were not always looking for the exit sign. They are highly energetic and protective of this energy. They are consistently motivated but prone to 'burnout' if not allowed space to breath and recover. If they find you interesting, they will come to you. If you find them annoying, leave them alone.

In a world that is changing too fast for the human mind to cope with, we need to unite and protect each other. These are the people who will do it without your knowledge, without the need for praise or reward. They are special.

The System

Without the system where would we be?

Wandering hand in hand with your family.

I cannot lead myself I need to be led!

Said the infinite soul chained to his bed.

Of course I trust them they wouldn't do that?

Then why do you question those lizard twats?

But they know best, someone has to lead?

Lead you where? Through a cycle of greed?

This is too deep I'm having a drink...

They want you subservient, not to think.

But I need my job I need to pay tax!

How's that working for you, still on the tracks?

I feel so depressed I don't know my purpose.

Neither do we, so come and join us.

But what can we do without their help?

We'll start by living,

Do some forgiving,

Together we'll figure it out.

This is not an academic book, this is just one mans thoughts. Through my own psychospiritual research and development I have realised that the further I study and try to explain this modern existence we find ourselves in; the further I remove my spiritual and political beingness from societal constraints. This kind of isolation is not for the faint of heart and mind. I advise spending periods of time with family members and members of your community who are avid lovers of the systems I am about to explain. This is your best source of grounding; a progressively humbling experience that will ground you but hopefully not affect you as you observe as a voyeur and play a role that has lost its purpose. I try my best to cover all aspects without prejudice but this topic is bound to be biased. As a man I have suffered from forms of abuse from the justice system, the police, my own family, my teachers and so on... I am not bitter and I am not alone. We all have our story to tell and yes, maybe I do want you the reader to question everything you are being told and have ever been taught. I hope this illuminates a few of your core ideals, perhaps you will re-evaluate them and start to think, feel and live in a way that feels more natural and harmonious to your physical environment and not just your community (a word regularly used but not understood). If we can change the way we feel as adults and regain the ability to think for ourselves then our children will surely benefit.

Sophie Scholl was executed in 1943 for leading a student resistance against Hitler. She was 21. Her last words were: "How can we expect righteousness to prevail when there is hardly anyone willing to give himself up individually to a righteous cause? Such a fine sunny day, and I have to go, but what does my death matter, if through us thousands of people are awakened and stirred to action?"

Ask yourself how this makes you feel? I am not trying to trick you into feeling emotion, these are the last words of a young lady during a war. If you will, please read it again...

Sophie was a member of The White Rose resistance movement of 1942 in Nazi Germany. Consisting of brave men who rose up and fought against the regime and the lesser known but equally brave resistance by it's women. They were students and professors of Germany's universities; they took up a non-violent opposition to the Nazi party. Their leaflets were provocative and very dangerous considering the politics at a time where philosophical books were burnt and people were silenced by execution or arrested for merely speaking badly of Adolf Hitler and his murderous war mongering.

She was a resistance activist who stood against an evil regime, she was not anti-government or an anarchist. She gave her life fighting for a cause that she believed was greater than her self. And this is the issue I find in our world that we live in today. Too often I speak to young men in their early twenties, full of pride and energy, wishing that Guy Fawkes had finished the job or that angry mobs would take arms and overthrow our 'evil' governments. If change comes through anarchy, then what comes after… "Anarchy is not a state of chaos, it is the absence of a hierarchical power structure." - Peter Kropotkin. Without a dominating authority how do you keep peace in a society of millions or even billions of souls? At what point do we lose the personal freedoms, supposed safety and security that our families live under? What happens after the fall of these overlords that govern us? Could we all survive without a system of control, is this what everyone wants?

"If I can't dance, I don't want to be part of your revolution." - Emma Goldman.

Small steps… as individuals, that is my answer. It is not yours, it is just my concept. If we sprint into change we do not get to see the scenery as it whizzes past us. The learning is always in the journey and not in the destination. I would like to walk with you on a journey that I hope will inspire you to want a change but not necessarily a violent one. As Martin Luther King said, "violence begets violence", but I am not one who turns the other cheek. "If you want to make an omelette, you have to break a few eggs." - George Danton.

Societal control is a system of mechanisms that regulate human behaviour and maintain social order. From research and my own experience I have found the system includes both formal and informal methods:

Formal social control

These are legally recognised and implemented by authorised (by themselves) agencies and individuals. Examples include:

- Laws and legislation: These are written declarations that define what is considered acceptable behaviour.
- Police: The primary agency responsible for maintaining law and order.
  Courts and legal systems: Use legal rules to determine cases and decide punishments.
- Prisons and correctional facilities: Used to punish and rehabilitate people who have broken the law.

This is based on belief systems learnt through socialisation, the:

Informal Social Control or 'Socialisation'

Examples include:

- Rewards and punishments: Family, friends, teachers and other members of society use these to program belief systems in children and peers.
- Sanctions: These can include shame, ridicule, criticism, disapproval and social exclusion.

I believe 'socialisation' is key here… This is the process by which people learn the values, norms and culture of a society. Through a combination of being taught and self-learning, it helps us to form our identity and function within a community.

There are two types of socialisation:

Primary socialisation: From birth we instinctively take on the values and behaviours of our close family. As children we must conform to these values in order to be accepted by our families. Deviation from the norm and you are cast as the 'black sheep' or 'problem child', destined to failure and judged from a very early age by those who should know better.

Secondary socialisation: During our early school years and throughout out teens, through our friendship groups and the government led education system. Peer pressure and the system are at war in this part of our socialisation. The one you feed the most will determine the winner. There is always a chance you were anti-social and anti-education and if so welcome brothers and sisters together, we shall unite!

Joking aside… you may be unravelling the bigger picture for yourself but I will go a little bit further on our journey, there are a few more mountains to climb…

Once we are accepted within a community, our children (if any) are integrated within the school system, we have become accepted as useful and friendly parents or adults. We are no longer a threat to the system. We are the system and we become the self-policing authority with the rest of the system that is to judge any newcomers to the community with rigorous tenure. It is in essence self-perpetuating and incredibly powerful. However, it is a choice…

A year ago my family moved 700 miles to the North West Coast of the Scottish Highlands, our dream of repatriating to our ancestral home of Scotland, both my wife and myself being of Irish and Scottish heritage. We had already had been home educating our eldest while our youngest was at nursery (which we see as more 'playing with other toddlers' than 'secondary socialisation') and also a chance for us as the head of our little family, to meet like minded parents and build honest friendships.

Moving to a very small community of 230 adults was a huge culture shock for us. No more anonymity, no more hiding amongst the crowds of busy towns and cities; the village we left in the middle of England had a population of over 2000 and was deemed to be fairly average in size for the area.

A few weeks before our 'big move' we had a bit of a dilemma. All of the brilliant reasons for home-educating our children for their betterment with the benefits of living around cities and towns with a plethora of amenities, extra-curricular classes and culture; all of this would disappear. We realised we would be left with only the community. The nearest small town (with one supermarket) an hours drive and the nearest city (Inverness) 2 hours away. We found ourselves having a fear of our children suffering from exclusion within this small community and decided to give the system a small chance purely for our eldest to gain friends and for us as adults to have a chance of being accepted by the community.

The social implications speak for themselves. Our daughter and son were recognised and accepted by the community. As parents we were accepted as well although living on the fringe and being of 'fringe' thoughts and ideals meant we were subject to the usual queries and fear. All in all an informative and rewarding experience. After a year of government-led schooling our daughter has chosen to do home education. We do not like to call it school. She has nicknamed it 'The MacLire Mystical Warrior Academy' and although I am not a fan of the uniforms of the Prussian school system there may be a cool logo and t-shirt on the way!

Our programming runs so deep that we automatically push our innocent children straight into the network without question. From a young age we ask them what they want to be when they grow up, we have our own ideas of what we think they should be; a doctor, a dentist, famous actor etc. We tell them they have to work hard at school, do as they're told, behave within acceptable parameters. We only notice that which aligns with our current beliefs. We observe our current experiences but we judge this experience only with the framework of reality that has been taught to us.

Any requests for change are usually met with redundancy; any small change would have to be implemented throughout every school, hospital or prison.

It is and always will be a matter of funding or lack thereof. As parents who have lost our eldest in primary school for the past year, we have found this unbearably frustrating. The parent-council meetings were absolutely pointless, even small changes like having a lock on the school gates due to them opening up to a main road were agreed but never implemented. The larger issues of bullying and lack of staff for due diligence of care were met with 'we don't have the funding'. Is it pointless to have your say as a parent? I don't think it is, I just think there is another way...

If we illuminate the issues within our communities aside from governing bodies, however small your community may be. We start our own groups of parents who want change in the system, write reports in as much detail as possible; what is lacking, the resulting issues and what you would like to see change in the very near future. Perhaps also the threat of children leaving the system if the issue is not resolved immediately. Take this report straight to your local MP. Use social media groups to spread the word and gain support from people who may still be under the thumb of the system. As individuals we should matter, but to the system we are insignificant. Together we are an army, alone we are a target.

If you gain the support of the public, you have already won. Those who work within the system to keep it alive are but few, the real power lies within the population. We pay the taxes, we pay their wages. We place them in these positions of power so that they can implement our requests so bloody well use them. It is and always will be a numbers game. Get the numbers behind your cause. With a thousand small communities behind you, you will have a million people. You can be heard and we will listen. Together we can make the small changes needed to improve our children's present and future lives and help to empower the voices of those who have been silenced by each other.

Unite, find common ground, this is our home, our future.

What is the system? Just a bunch of conspiracy theories? It is right in front of us, it does not hide. We are just taught to ignore it from an early age. Once you become the hamster on the wheel you will just keep buying time and energy keeping the system running.

The system is alive and has consciousness. It relies on your subservience, your sheep mentality. It wants us to be in large nucleated populations under watchful eye. It wants to be an automated program where the humans are the product, the workforce, the oil and the blood. Without you the system would not work. Without you there would be no need for 'The System'.

From the second you were born and and if your name was written on your Birth Certificate, you had been signed away into a contract with the system. Registration of cars, houses, births and marriage are all contracts that hold words and words are powerful. We give our power away willingly and without question and then we give our children to the system we have empowered. It is an endless cycle and it feels unnatural because it is.
Even if you believe we are all souls living a human experience and not just humans who have souls; can you remember a life without this system? If you claim to have lived many lives on Earth can you tell me how it felt to be under the martial law of territories split by

small kingdoms prior to governments, (supposedly) elected by the people?

I think that for myself, I dream of a world were we can have the ideals of peaceful, tribal (communal) living where:

- Local farms feed local people
- Local trees are used for local building,
- Our children are educated by parents and the elders of the community not by strangers, they spend more time with their family than their friends.
- The local community is the heart and soul of the collective or tribe.

Perhaps some changes can be made from within instead of without. If we work on our inner-world we will be in a stronger position to change our outer-world. Your brain is a filter dependent on your conditioning. Our neural pathways strengthen with use much like a muscle strengthens with repetitive exercise. This is why we call it muscle memory. The more you perform a complex task the easier it becomes until eventually it will be as automatic as walking.

This neuroplasticity can be a gift and a curse, it depends on what you feed it. If you believe you are an insignificant cog in the machine (or system of societal control), you will automatically function within these parameters. Your ego will play along and will defend this safe 'reality' you live in from any possible threats.

I only started to be conscious of this after making small changes in my daily routine. For example, from doing no morning self-care whatsoever I forced myself to wake up at 5am and practice an hour of yoga every day for a year. Within a few weeks the practice became a habit and all aspects of my life saw huge benefits. My relationships with my wife and my children became more important to me than they had before. I became more aware of where I focussed my mind and energy in the present moment. I became present.

When I took a shower, I had a shower. I felt the water cleansing my body and I stopped planning my day ahead.

When playing with my daughter, I put my phone down, I became aware of her attention and how much she valued my own.

Yoga is just an example, there are many practices that can help you become more present, less reactive and more responsible for your own wellbeing. I cannot and will not underestimate the value of this anymore. It is not just good practice, it is essential for your own personal evolution and the evolution of our species beyond this mess we find ourselves in. Our disconnect from nature, our souls and each other has taken its toll. We are becoming part of a machine that has too little oil to function and is breaking from the inside out. Let your consciousness become part of the neuroplasticity, let your awareness be ever present within the present and you will become the observer of your actions and start to experience life outside of your mental chatter.

This to me is heaven. Becoming our true nature, becoming the awareness not the mental imagery. Your brain has an automated intelligence just as your heart and lungs do. They all function automatically without our attention so stop giving your brain and its thoughts the incessant analysis it does not require or deserve.

We all love to hate 'memes' but occasionally one pops up on your socials and you know you have to share it. Being the unaware but loyal part of this 'System' is also how they get away with forcing us to remain in our homes and giving many of us no options other than taking untested, suspicious money laundering vaccines. I pray to the Gods that they try that one again, it would break the system and they know it. The next attack will come in a different guise, I expect the threat of alien invasion, killer meteor or something similarly dramatic… Whatever 'they' believe is necessary to convince the world to unite under their New World Order. We shall see. In the meantime I shall end with this quote from Rudolf Steiner (1861-1925), an Austrian occultist, esotericist and the founder of Anthroposophy:

"In the future, we will eliminate the soul with medicine. Under the pretext of a 'healthy point of view', there will be a vaccine by which the human body will be treated as soon as possible directly at birth, so that the human being cannot develop the thought of the existence of Soul and Spirit.

To materialistic doctors, will be entrusted the task of removing the soul of humanity. As today, people are vaccinated against this disease or that disease, so in the future, children will be vaccinated with a substance that can be produced precisely in such a way that people, thanks to this vaccination, will be immune to being subjected to the 'madness' of spiritual life.

He would be extremely smart, but he would not develop a conscience, and that is the true goal of some materialistic circles.

With such a vaccine, you can easily make the etheric body loose in the physical body.

Once the etheric body is detached, the relationship between the universe and the etheric body would become extremely unstable, and man would become an automaton, for the physical body of man must be polished on this Earth by spiritual will.

So, the Vaccine becomes a kind of arymanique force; man can no longer get rid of a given materialistic feeling. He becomes materialistic of constitution and can no longer rise to the spiritual."

Healing Tools

Through busy days and sleepless nights,
I search for answers, claw and fight.
For never will I truly know,
How to listen, learn and grow.
You see my greatest enemy,
Is not without, it is in me.
My greatest chance of letting go,
Is at war with my ego.

I feel its time to be at peace,
To find some comfort and release.
Perhaps I'll find some peace in time,
Through healers hired and students' minds
Until then I'll claw and fight,
Through busy days and sleepless nights.
Until the cycle does evolve,
I'll never learn, I'll never solve.

I cannot share many of the tools I have learnt so far. They are not mine to share and I have been asked not to by most of my mentors. This is not just about giving knowledge away for free when there should be reciprocity. It is not just because of the respect I feel towards my mentor's teachings. This is about the realisation that "With great power comes great responsibility" - Voltaire. The New International Version of the Bible states - "From everyone who has been given much, much will be demanded; and from the one who has been entrusted with much, much more will be asked".

This is not a text book on Shamanic Healing and I have not the knowledge or experience to teach such esoteric arts as of yet. I know I am a teacher at heart and one day this will take shape into a course of sorts. I will perhaps teach my version of healing (or a blend of one created with my wife) on our retreat space in Badcall Bay. For now I feel it is right to share some of the tools I have adapted and I regularly use in my own spiritual self-care. When I have my practice of self-care right: my physical health, my relationships with the outside world, my family and in particular my children look and feel more aligned, healthy and honest. If this is something that you feel might help you then please read on. I have said before, If you need further help then please reach out. If I cannot help you myself I know many humble healers with kind hearts who may be able to get you back to 50%.

And that is the secret… true healing is and should always be about getting your client or yourself back to 50%. Once we are half way there with the help of others, or self-healing tools, the rest of the healing will happen naturally. Guided by the intuition of our souls, our conscious, subconscious and superconscious states and the intelligence of our bodies; we all have the power to heal ourselves. Why would we want to disempower others by saying they need us to heal them? I do not have the answer to that, but maybe you have witnessed your self or others offering healing to those that have not asked for it?

I recently caught up with a new friend of mind called Daniel at a seaweed conservation event in a local Village in the Highlands. Never one to enjoy small talk, we went straight into the deep dive (how refreshing). Although he is on a very connected spiritual journey, his life (like mine) has been filled so far with such varied experiences that I value his wisdom and intuition. When asked how I should advertise my healing business and retreat his response resonated very deeply: "Jordan... advertising and marketing are the solution to a problem. The problem is nobody wants what you are selling them so you have to trick them into thinking they need what you are selling'. Let that sink in... I will never try and persuade you that you need my help, everyone needs *some* form of healing from time to time. I have received and continue to get mine through learning healing modalities.

The practice of learning how to heal others is full of practicing each type of healing with other students. In order to know how to heal others safely you need to practice and receive healing yourself under the guidance of a mentor. I remember feeling so overly healed after a year of intensive counselling training that I swore I would never need CBT[8] again. I was wrong, but it certainly helped to heal some old wounds.

Here are a few tricks and tips to get you back on track or as additions to your current self-care. Some will be fairly obvious to many of you but these simple methods can often be the most fruitful. Maybe it is time to revisit them? My aim here is not to teach you or to get too specific, just to inspire and perhaps help you to see what may resonate. Each one of these healings has been written about more than I would find the time to read...

Grounding in nature/ Forest bathing

This has become a cliche in a never-ending stream of memes, but still remains the most simple and rewarding of any tools I could recommend to anyone (even those who are not on a spiritual path). The simple act of taking a walk or sitting in meditation without distractions through or in land and preferably ancient woodland, is hugely rewarding.

---

8 Cognitive Behavioural Therapy - or 'talking therapy'.

After a complicated healing for a client, a difficult conversation that has given me an emotional response, after being triggered in a way that I cannot shake off; I find that a walk in a woodland or away from society in a wild open space is always beneficial. One walk or meditation in nature will not cure you of depression, but it will (especially if you ask the trees and nature spirits) release those daily anxieties and help your 'pain body'[9] weaken to a more comfortable state.

Energy Healing

I have not specifically titled this as Reiki, but Reiki is the obvious practice. This is the easiest spiritual healing practice to learn and use to help yourself and others. There are three levels and each can be reached in just a weekend (each) of training (although there are rules about the time between training to the next level).
If you have heard about this and it resonates, I would just go straight in for the training at level 1. I believe it is a very gentle introduction into the spiritual world. Many

---

[9] Eckhart Tolle's description of the energy field of repressed emotion that many people carry.

of the people I trained with were not particularly spiritually minded, although years later it seems that learning Reiki was the beginning of their exploration into the esoteric.

What I love about Reiki is also why I do not practice it on my clients (even though I am at level 2). It is simple and it can be very effective. However, for me there is a resounding feeling that it may be a bit too 'fluffy'. I guess I like my healing to really get deep and dark into our shadow side. I do not believe in quick fixes, you get out what you put in.

It is not a criticism but it feels too rigid with its symbolism and too centred on its founder for my liking. I do not fixate on any one practice and I do not worship anything or anyone; this fluidity has served me well. Do what feels right for you…

Learning Healing Modalities

As I have said before… learning how to heal others has been a deeply rewarding process.

I have spent a lot of time surrounded by student healers. In one particular counselling course we would spend one weekend of the month on eight hour Zoom calls with 20 to 30 students. It was a rolling course that you could start at any time and if you missed a module you could do it again the next time it came back around. Even so, I made some close connections to some special souls, especially with those who had started the 14 module course at the same time as myself. This level of healing not only gave me a healthy and humble confidence in my abilities but also healed me good and proper!

Find a mentor

But do not settle for anyone that does not feel right. I have started a 12 module course because the content was ideal, only to stop by module 2 because the energy of the mentor did not align with mine.

Once a training is complete I always find it beneficial to find another mentor or start another course. Not only is it a humbling experience to empty your cup and become a student again, it is also rewarding to gain wisdom from mentors and build close connections with like-minded students.

Quite often those on a spiritual path can be left feeling isolated, we are a bit different are we not? It is so refreshing to be in a safe circle of learning with other souls, I always find it invigorating. Being a perpetual student can also lead to burnout. I recommend taking a year or so to process lessons and let the work integrate.

Seek a healer

There is an abundance of them just a local google search away. I would suggest asking friends if they know any first as there is nothing more powerful than a word of mouth recommendation; sspecially when you realise the often sinister and manipulative power of advertising campaigns and the algorithms that seduce us.

The question is what kind of healing do you need and are comfortable with? There is an awful lot to choose from. Whichever direction you go, whether it is a Reiki , Shamanism, Past Life Regression or QHHT; all practitioners (should) work with the same universal source energy for the higher good of themselves and you the client.

Everyone needs to gain experience but do not be afraid to ask them how much they have. Wisdom is important, and has been forgotten and replaced by angst and casual ignorance. I feel I may digress here but is an important point. We now live in a world where the younger generation believe that texting someone is talking to them, that you can solve life's riddles by watching a ten minute YouTube video and true happiness depends on your monetary wealth.

I realise this is a generalisation but it is now a common theme.

Before the dawn of the written word and keeping of ledgers, all knowledge was passed down from generation to generation through the spoken word and practical mentorship.

Something I believe to be important when choosing a healer; Ask them if they too seek healing. If they say no then it is up to you whether or not you wish to receive healing from someone who believes they are complete. I am not saying that everyone needs to be in turmoil, but perhaps an honest healer will know that even they require help and guidance from other practitioners from time to time?

Chanting of Galdr, Magik of Seidr

I am writing a small book that explains the use of the Elder Futhark runes for divination and for the casting and chanting of spells. This should be available some time this year (2025) but in the meantime please refer to the 'further reading' page at the end of this book for some brilliant guides to the runes.

The runes are not dissimilar to a Tarot deck when used for divination but the training required to use them safely should be taken very seriously.

In the wrong hands a deep knowledge of the runes can be very dangerous. I like to compare a seasoned caster to a master of martial arts. The more they know the less aggressive methods they feel they need to use.

There have been a few instances in my life where I have used the runes for cursing or as a reaction to somebodies behaviour. Not only is this an irresponsible use of power but it is also at a high risk. The wisdom of the runes is far greater than any one persons practice and they have a tendency to back fire on the practitioner if you are not being just.

Yoga, Qigong, Tai chi or any form of somatic healing.

I can speak from first hand experience when I say that Yoga is an incredibly powerful tool for the body and the mind. For one year without fail I would wake up at 5am and do up to an hour of yoga. The serenity I felt during this year was obvious in my demeanour, posture, radiance and toned body. Ironically to reconnect to nature and our ancestral home we moved our family to a wee Croft house in the wild North West Coast of Scotland. Here I have no space tall or wide enough to practice in, I have lost my practice, but not forever... Yoga is not just about stretching your body and becoming comfortable in positions that seem unnatural; it is about finding peace of mind and an unfocussed tranquility through the medium of movement and most importantly smooth and rhythmical breathing. It is also a practice and not a perfection. Even seasoned yogis are still improving and adjusting their practice.

Affirmations, Confirmations, Prayers and Mantras

This is not a robotic process. You cannot just speak the words and expect results, your heart is alive, it responds to feelings and energy. Give it more than just a thought. You have to truly believe in something, to really feel into it. Gratitude and respect to whatever you wish for or are asking help from are key here.

The removal of the words 'want' and 'need' will help you get the results that you seek. The universe will provide. If you constantly 'want' and 'need' then that is what you shall receive. You will never have anything because that would relinquish your need.

Some examples: I have a morning prayer of gratitude for this life with a call to the four directions[10]. It leaves me grounded and ready for the day ahead. When working with Gods or goddesses of the Hindu religion such as Maha Kali; I have practiced month long repetitive chantings of certain mantras. The effects have been obvious and noticeable. Again, you get out what you put in. Do not expect results without a real

---

[10] See chapters: 'Four Direction Blessings' and 'Morning Prayers'.

commitment and please try and dive deeper than YouTube for your information. I still watch it for research but it is becoming difficult to differentiate between what information is real (from a human) and what is Artificial Intelligence.

Quantum Healing Hypnotherapy Technique or QHHT.

This practice quite literally changed my life. I did at least a year of research before going for my first session. Thankfully I was able to switch off my discerning left brain and relax into a beautiful journey through past-lives and the cosmos. Too much research can make it very difficult to not to judge the process and the practitioner.

This is a deep diving technique. I loved the research as much as the actual healing. It is based on the guided hypnosis technique perfected over 40 years of practice by the late Dolores Canon. With 17 substantial books published, each full of transcripts from her years of practice. Although her work is very much on the 'fringe' of many belief systems, it is none the less stimulating.

What hooked my attention was the abundance of coincidences and repetitive results and stories from her clients with no contact with each other (being from opposite sides of the world). Her books are huge. I have had to listen to many of them (through lack of time) on Audible whilst doing simple chores, they are very addictive and helped me to have more of an open mind if anything.

With or without the research I would recommend finding a practitioner and diving into this fascinating world. It took to me distant planets, a life as a plant and an extremely emotional and rewarding 'memory' of being at Source without an ego. The gift of feeling this universal connection has stuck with me, it has definitely changed this life's course for the betterment of myself and others.

If anything please remind yourself not to heal in isolation, healing happens in community. With humans or with Spirit. The need to heal is the realisation that a hurt has taught you all that it needs to, now it needs to fall away. I hope I always have some darkness to heal from and while living, my path of learning never ends.

Hello Darkness My Old Friend

The deep dives get deeper,

You start to really see;

The twisting, snaking energy of hidden enemies.

They try to take what isn't theirs,

But you are wiser still,

They squirm inside your spirit self,

Its time to bay the bill.

Compassion is your greatest love,

Its kryptonite to them,

The colour drains, the smirk remains,

But soon you know they'll ken.

Subtle manipulations and mind games are not your playground, be honest with your words and your intentions.

Without making excuses for my way of thinking; in order to move along we have to make a few assumptions. By now I am hoping that you the reader has realised that I do not have opinions or motivations based on flippancy or ignorance. I have worked and continue to work as hard as I can to broaden my conscious landscape. By meticulously reading all sides available for every argument, diving deep into my own shadow work in my own subconscious mind and drawing from my ancestral and spiritual guides. I continue to grow and my 'base-line' for understanding and navigating through this life is constantly shifting; as I learn more I understand less and that is okay.

However, there is a method to teaching that although I find infuriating now that I have learnt a fair amount; I now realise that it is crucial. You cannot go from being an amateur to an expert overnight. You cannot expect to be able to intuit the feelings of a crowd of people and complex networking of their energy and emotions if you have only just started a spiritual path. Good luck to you if you think you can, you could end up very ill very soon. I have tried to open up to energies way beyond my skill in the past, the inevitable burnout and sectioning in a 'mental health' institute was a very tough pill to swallow (metaphorically and physically). It took me back to square one.

My persistence and stubbornness would not stop me until I had been through this process 5 times through 15 years of esoteric exploration. It was only when I realised that the pain I was causing those around me was far greater than the intuitive lessons I was gaining; only then did I stop punishing myself by repeating cycles of self-abuse in an attempt to gain self-awareness and self-love. My biggest revelation was that there really is nothing other than consciousness. There is no heaven or hell, no good or bad, names, physicality; nothing... but a perception or awareness of your surroundings through sensory experiences, thoughts and language.

I do not believe humans are the only intelligent species on this planet, we are unique but so is every other species. I do believe that "where focus goes, energy flows"; that we are the creators of our consciousness and everything that we perceive. If every human is unconsciously aware that they are a conscious creature then welcome to hell on Earth!

So do I believe in evil? Yes and no. As children we are taught the concepts of good and evil, right and wrong. Christians are taught to personify good and evil into God or Jesus versus the Devil or his minions. They are also taught that if you are good, upon death you will go to heaven and if you are bad you will go to hell. I hope you can see where this is going. If you believe in these concepts then you will manifest them in your life and potentially in your death as well...

I have come to understand that good and evil, everything and nothing in infinite variety only exists within myself and not without. Everything is subjective so objectivity is the only way of being at true peace with it all. In other words, a lack of bias, judgement or prejudice for anything that exists external to our own perception is the only method I have found for accepting life in its ebbs and flows. Your strongest tool against evil is looking inside your self and bringing your buried emotions and thoughts to the surface. You can read ten books a week, write daily blogs, wax lyrical; you can be the smartest man or women in the room. Unless you have searched within yourself and accepted that part of you we like to call our shadow self, you are just being clever without an ounce of real intelligence.

Real wizardry, real magik exists. I have witnessed it so often that I now practice it without incantations, ceremonies, or second thoughts. Once you break down the barriers that only exist within your mind it is incredible just how powerful we all are. You cannot and should not expect this to happen without hard work. If you take shortcuts there will be consequences. We have all heard of the conspiracy theories of some famous musicians 'selling their souls to the devil' in order to gain fame and fortune.

If you want to gain true power then stop looking for it. If you want to learn how to be happy then be comfortable being angry, and sad. Dig deep into the parts of yourself that you have pushed so far into your subconscious that only in your dreams they scream at you to be heard. Learn to let these parts come into the light of your conscious mind. Be the 'observer', know that your shadow self is there to give you a complete experience in this life.

I took the subject of Biology at school from a young age up to A-level (pre-College or University level). We learnt the structure and function of an individual cell so that under exam conditions we could answer questions and draw diagrams to show we could listen in class and access this learning under pressure. Every time we went to the next level of learning (in the UK, from GCSE's to A-level's for example) we were told that everything we had learnt before was actually wrong. We would start again from the beginning and the learning and understanding would be deeper and more complex. This method of learning presumed we were ready for this understanding because we had prepared for it in our previous learning.

It looks like I was lied to, but was I not just being taught to follow a process of learning that would teach me how to understand complexities that would have baffled my younger mind had I jumped straight into the teachers current understanding of the cell? Interestingly, the teachers' knowledge would be at least a couple of academic levels higher than mine so they would be fully aware that they were educating us with false information.

If it seems like I am not making a point here, this is it…
If you are looking for answers through a mentor, a teacher, a book, a podcast, your parents, then you will learn lessons (subject to the level they choose) that is certain, but they will never stop and they will not be yours to learn. Look within.

How do we look within?
I started with meditation. Sitting in a quiet room away from external noise, I would sometimes listen to theta brain wave tracks or Shamanic drum tracks to induce a trance state. These would inevitably turn into Shamanic journeys and that is a different story for another time! It

was during quiet times of meditation that I would receive clear and sometime amusing tit bits from Source. I remember one time in particular whilst driving to work through local countryside I saw a Barn Owl flying next to my truck. It flew with me for far longer than I felt was normal. I was so inspired by this sight that I called my wife and asked her to check our 'Animal Spirit Guides' book (by Steven D. Farmer) for a spiritual explanation. The message was clear. Smudge your home and take some time to have some quiet reflection.

It had been a tumultuous time for us as a family. A time of letting go of old and unsettling ties and a time to reflect inwards and take stock of how fortunate we were to have each other. The stress however, had taken its toll and there was a dark feeling in our home that we could not lift.

It had been some time since we had smudged the house and it was a fun process to do as a family. I love the smell of burning white sage. We opened every cupboard door and window to make sure the whole house was cleansed. Next came the quiet meditation.

After putting the kids to bed I sat in our study with noise reducing headphones, lights off laying back in a comfy chair. After about twenty minutes of relative peace and just before I decided to bring myself back; a topless, bald, humanoid figure appeared as a vision. He was dancing flamboyantly with a big smile on his face. He stopped, turned towards me and quite clearly sang in a Jim Carry type voice: 'cosmic intervention!'. I burst out laughing, he disappeared and I thanked him and Source for giving me presence of mind. This was all that I needed.

Now for some practical magik if I may... Please know that people enter your etheric body and take or manipulate your energy more often than you think. They do this without your knowledge and mostly without their own.

They take others' energy and leave them depleted because they have no idea of their own blockages and power. Sadly some people do know what they are doing. Hopefully you will have become intuitively aware of the warning signs. You are a peaceful warrior but you are still a Warrior…

If being around certain people makes you irritable but you feel that you have no choice but an obligation to be in their company; take this as an opportunity to practice being present. Instead of spending days dreading their company and how they make you feel, try and wait until you meet. Be the one who witnesses that feeling that arises and instead of reacting to this and wallowing in the emotion. This is now when you make a choice to:

• Find exactly where you feel it on your body.
• Analyse this feeling. Turn it from an emotion into a physical ball in your imagination. Keep it exactly where you found it.
• Now see a red glowing string of energy flowing from their sacral centre (groin area) into your etheric energy (auric field) and surrounding this physical ball of emotion.
• Connect into the infinite energy of the all Source, God, Creator etc. Whichever suits you. I do this by imagining a golden beam of light energy beaming

down from my own personal star above me into the top of my head and filling me with this infinite supply of energy. This is crucial, do not try and use your own energy you will simply be giving it away and will quickly exhausted.

- Now surround the red energy and the emotional ball in your body with this golden pure energy and watch as the red energy instantly weakens. Continue by pushing their red energy outside of your auric field and surround yourself with your golden, protective, Source energy.

There are ways to throw this attack back to its source and to weaken it but this is dangerously close to dark magik. I have used this defensive attack before and since realised it would be totally unnecessary if I knew how to protect myself properly in the first instance. You may be channeling pure golden universal energy into someone but I do not condone healing people without their permission. This is for those moments where you know you are being attacked and you suspect they understand the energy behind it.

I would not call it dark magik but it is not light, there is an in-between, a grey area that I believe should only be used when all other options have been exhausted. There is a lot of magik that falls into this area, a lot of magik that I would not share; this kind becomes quite natural to those who practice their crafts regularly and do the work. You have to earn this and I will never write it down. It is far too tempting for those who are being persecuted.

Be careful how you practice, do not start throwing your energy around. You will find it will disappear and without knowledge you will be using your own limited source. You will feel like you have been sapped of energy because you have given it all away to the person who has energetically attacked you.

Why does this power disappear? For the same reason that many of us have lost our connection to each other. If we choose power over compassion there will be blockages in you Chakras, in particular the higher Chakras from Anahata (heart) to Sahasrara (the crown). This happens because we become unbalanced from within.

After any encounter of this kind always remember to ground yourself with a glass of water, take your socks off and put your feet on some soil. Alternatively walk near or through a woodland. The trees will ground you and are home to spirits that will happily take any remnants of bad energy from you. Also remember to always ask the permission of the tree if you feel the need to touch them. Whatever you do, if you involve another Spirit give the gift of gratitude, it is the least we can do. Offerings work best and you should use your intuition to know what and how to give them. Above all remember that "Warriors aren't born, and they aren't made. They create themselves through trial and error and by their ability to conquer their own frailties and faults" - Philip J. Messina.

Becoming 'The Witness' Not 'The Worry'

I need to make that call, I haven't paid that bill,
Where's the day gone, I've no time to kill.
It's getting late and I haven't done the dishes,
I'll just have a drink, they're tomorrows wishes.

I can't believe they did that when I was a bairn,
They say that they loved me but caused me such harm.
They'll never change, the future looks bleak,
I'll give them a call, I'll give it a week.

So much chatter within our heads,
It takes all your time, awake and in bed.
Try not think about letting thoughts go,
Just chill the 'f' out and go with the flow.

Overthinking... I have fallen into this trap more often than not. I still do but I am aware of it, I am its witness.

Isn't it funny that the people I know who are on a similar spiritual path feel that they suffer from this more than they did before their first 'Aha!' moments.

I believe that they are actually benefitting (not suffering) from a greater awareness of their own thoughts, that they have become or are becoming more aware of their thoughts as separate to who (or what) they really are. Ironically, they may be overthinking about their thoughts which is very confusing.

In order to become enlightened I believe you have to deeply realise this existential truth; to transcend your thoughts you have to at first witness them in order to let them go.

When we witness our thoughts where are we witnessing them from? Your awareness (consciousness) is the witness. It witnesses your body, mind, feelings etc. It does not control them they have their own intelligence. When your body heals from an injury, who is doing the healing? Your body is. It has its own intelligence and will heal itself with or without its witness.

Who controls your mind? The answer is your mind does. If you are really in control then try and stop your mind from thinking… There are grey areas here, there are some Buddhist monks that have mastered their minds and egos to the point of being able to heat their bodies at will, heal faster, do other miraculous things us normal folk could only dream of. I have not witnessed this but I believe it is possible. I would recommend starting small but do not limit yourself. I have no ides what you are capable of, as far as I know you are a demi-god or one of the Aesir living a human life. I believe we have infinite potential, our beautifully crafted bodies are the perfect house for our infinitely powerful souls. Do not give your attention to mediocrity, you will suffocate your growth and talk about the weather for the rest of your life (note to self - 'I talk about the weather A LOT!').

If you have a meditation practice of any kind you may have trained yourself to witness the thoughts that appear in your mind and just let them go. If you allow these thoughts to claim your attention you give them power. If you give them power then they will control you.

If your thoughts are separate to who you are then who is the witness witnessing them, who is letting them go? You are the you that is not thinking, the witness of the thoughts. The you that is connected to something it does not try and explain. The part of you that knows without questioning. This is the you that lives entirely in the present moment, aware that time does not exist and that while you are having a shower, you are having a shower. The water feels amazing as each droplet splashes against your skin, cleansing you from accumulated physical and spiritual stowaways. But then, from the argument that you had with your spouse, or the stern word you had with your daughter, "was I too hard on her, maybe I should have been a little bit calmer?" These thoughts arise and demand your attention.

What do you do? Absolutely nothing, just continue to have a shower. Do not reminisce the past day or plan your day ahead ("but I always plan my day when I have a shower in the morning"). I promise you this, the most important take away here is that if you never ever plan your day you will still get everything done just the same. Do you truly believe that our brilliant minds have not already figured out exactly what they have to do by now. Do you think about how you walk, eat, drive, write, communicate etc...

I remember a family skiing trip to France, I was sixteen and getting to grips with snowboarding. It was the last run of the day, the sun was setting and the ski lifts had stopped their steady flow up the mountain. I had struggled to get to to grips with boarding on this trip. I was pretty good on ski's, I could go off piste and although I had no real finesse I was fast and able to keep up with the best of them. The jump-down in skill from a seasoned skier to newby boarder was frustrating. I had the distinct fear of missing out.

I clicked my free boot into its binding, sat and waited for the rest of the party to set off from the top of the slope.

I remember looking at the orange glow of the setting sun between two peaks as I carved my way down the mountain. I was a little bit taken back by the beauty of this landscape before me. The suns waning glow was magical and made the snow twinkle and come alive. All I could hear was the sound of my board slicing tracks through the snow and the whistle of the cool air as I struggled to keep up with my party, all of whom were on two planks not one.

I was doing it! I was snow boarding! My awareness shifted its attention to my board, I started to think about what I was doing… within a second I 'caught an edge', wiped out and face planted the snow which at the bottom of the slope near the town was mostly ice. This was a painful lesson, one that I didn't learn from at the time. I am not saying let yourself be led like a robot or automaton through life. I am saying perhaps let the job you care little about and the basic functions, fear of being late, worry about what others think of you, let it all go… Give it a chance, you are missing so much life in this state of overthinking.

The less you do the more everything will fall into place. That does not mean that sitting idly all day will take care of your children, do the house work or your job. What it means is, let all the baggage surrounding your day to day 'chores' and your 'work' just drift away.

Let the Sunday fear, the worries about paying your bills this month, let all of them be present but do not feed them. Try and joke less about your stress and hardships, that only gives them power and creates a negative aura around you (regardless of how witty you may be).

If you say you are affected by the seasons, you will be affected by the seasons. If you say I have no money, you will have no money… the universe provides.

If you say you 'want' something, you will get what you asked for… you will continue to 'want' that thing and will never get it. Rather be grateful for what you have, say it out loud now and again.

'I am wealthy I have so much and am so grateful', if you say it enough you will believe it!

I no longer separate paid work from say doing the dishes, taking my dogs for a walk or playing with my kids. I do not hold them all at the same value or importance but I class them all as 'work' and I have learnt to love all of my 'work'. In fact I now consider my life as work and that feels good. I am always at work. I am always learning and growing at work.

No amount of reminiscing will change the past, it has gone, it no longer exists. It is only memory. If it does not serve your growth then make space for new ones. No amount of worry or fear will change the future, the future does not exist. Only the present exists and only the present can affect your life. This will absolutely change your life. If you can live like this for one day you will break so many bad habits. You will pause before entering into negative gossip when dropping off the kids at school. You will see where you are lacking as a parent, a friend, somebodies child. Most importantly and if you realise this, much of the rest will fall into place... you will see that you need to forgive yourself and be proud of who you are and what you have achieved. You are so so special. You are unique, nobody know you truly. Show us who you are, who you really are. We want to really see you, the you that hides behind societal constraints and small talk. Be brave, be the example. Be the change.

The more you realise you are the witness, the more you let go and let the 'intelligence' of your mind, body and nature do their best. You will witness just how fortunate you are.

If you have found this helpful in any way and wish to take the journey further, please read Eckhart Tolle's book 'A New Earth' and 'The Four Agreements' by Don Miguel Ruiz (after writing and editing this chapter I have realised this is almost the blurb to Eckhart's book!).

These two books have changed my life dramatically. I read and write as much as I can but I can honestly say that they give me new inspiration every time I re-read them. They are both on audiobooks as well, sometimes I find it is easier to listen while we let our muscle memory (our minds) do the mundane. I have listened to each of them over a dozen times.

Also please contact us if you want to discuss this. I am a trained Holistic Counsellor and my wife and I can provide many therapies that may be of help as well as our Animystic (Shamanic) healings.

Beware the 'Agent'

A Psychospiritual Thesis On Manipulative Behaviours

You've learnt that darkness is also your friend,
It helps you survive in this unwelcoming world.
The smiles that do not match the energy,
You have out worked these patterns through years of study.

You see now in others what you accept in yourself,
You don't need to challenge them, protect your own health.
A part of them knows they are laid bare in your witness,
So pause and observe while they learn their own lessons.

Are you emotionally intuitive, a Sigma, or a peaceful warrior but still struggling with inconsistent moods and your general health?

You may feel oppressed and often depressed with cycles and patterns that keep on repeating themselves.

Colleagues and trusted people within your circle may seem to turn against you and you are not sure what you have done. This may not come from within. Beware the 'Agent'.

Without sparking an irrational fear in you the reader, your best friend or family member could also be your worst enemy.

Disguised evil comes in many shapes and forms. When it resides within a soul it is quite literally a tangible and very physical means of manipulation. For the sake of this text and because it is culturally relevant we shall call them 'Agents' (from 'The Matrix' movie). If we are being a bit more playful we could call them schemers, conspirators, exporters or intriguers. Whatever we call them they are far more complex than a simple word. They have complicated layers of deceit, some so deep that in order for their manipulations to come to fruition they often truly believe their own lies.

Now before we delve into this topic, you may ask why I know so much about this and am I qualified in this area enough to give insight and opinion? The answers are yes and a resounding yes.

I have spent tens of thousands of hours studying the psychology of humanity and the psychology of philosophy. I have counselling qualifications (albeit spiritual ones) but none the less insurable and overlapping more clinical cognitive behavioural therapies. I have spent much of my life on a non-religious spiritual path which has also led me to the practice of Shamanism, which again has taken and continues daily to take (with pleasure and gratitude) a serious amount of my time, effort and energy. To be brutally honest, I have also been the Agent. There are no excuses, but as a child and young man I was surrounded at work and at home by abusive people who wanted me not to be me.

It is amazing what we do to survive physical and mental abuse. It is a common practice for the persecuted to find a victim to pass that persecution on to. I have been cheated on and passed on that pain. I have been emotionally bullied and passed it on. Nobody is a Saint, we can try our best and that is all we can do. The one thing I am certain of is that I absolutely will not intentionally abuse my power and manipulate others for personal gain. I have used some forms of manipulation in my spiritual work but only with the consent of clients and in a very controlled manner and mindset. On this note, we must be careful not to point fingers or ostracise those that we think are causing harm. As you will soon see, by shining a light on the Agents, the changes will happen naturally without the need for attacking them with the same negative energy that they thrive upon.

Rest assured, you are in safe hands; but 'be careful who you trust, salt and sugar look the same'. Not everyone that smiles at you is your friend. Perhaps I can give you some tools that may help you to distinguish the intentions of people who are in your (etheric) space. If you learn to read the signs outwardly and inwardly, life will be a smoother ride, of that I am sure.

Not everyone has finely tuned intuition, I quite often expect people to be able to do what I do and then I remember the time and effort I have put in. Trying to help people make sense of these subtle warning signs is frustrating when my major sensory skill is my intuition. Did you know the established theory that a dogs primary sense is its smell? They use their sight and hearing for confirmation. Humans have 6 million olfactory receptors in our noses, dogs typically have 300 million. When they come across a new smell they will find its source, see it, hear it and then give it a closer sniff to store that scent in their memory.

If my intuitive reading of a human does not match their physical expressions, the words that they say, their tone perceived inclination; I know that they are being dishonest. I am not a mind reader, usually I will just keep them at a safe distance, be polite but put my boundaries up. They may just be having a really bad day after all and I am not their judge and jury. If they are going to be in my etheric space for the foreseeable future and it becomes clear that they are an Agent... I do not give them any energy, I do not feed them with anything but compassion. I still find it is my duty to give people in the surrounding community the tools I believe may help them live their best lives. The phrase 'you can lead a horse to water but you can't make it drink' is my personally mantra in these situations.

Nobody is being forced to read this, you do so on your on accord, take from it what you will...

If you have you ever been introduced to an established circle of friends for the first time it can sometimes be a daunting experience as the outsider. You are invited by your new neighbour to meet a group of her friends in a local cafe. You are new to the area and although you are happy in your own skin you start to feel irrationally nervous. Will they like me? What should I say? Who is approachable? All very common thoughts we can empathise with. We often rush into quick judgements when we are in stressful situations. Humans have a habit of putting mental labels on new situations, it makes us feel safer when we make familiar the things that feel threatening.

When we are put under pressure out of our usual comfort zone, our attention is usually focussed on the person who is demanding it. Because, let's face it, you do not want all eyes on you, you'd rather just giggle away at the not so funny obnoxious person who is talking over everyone else.

Never judge anyone on your first impressions. First impressions are not important if you are a rounded individual on a path of wisdom. Any one of the protagonists on that table could have had a bad nights sleep, an argument with their spouse, a sick family member, be in debt; anything is possible so don't judge them for letting the loud one do all the talking. The Agent (in my experience) will not take long to make themselves known but do not jump to conclusions.

I struggle sometimes when meeting new people. I have spent an awful lot of time learning to read peoples energy. I am so sensitive to other peoples energy that only a decade ago I could not bare to be in a supermarket during busy times of the day. It felt like I was being attacked by bad moods, aggression and lethargy even if my own day was going particularly well. Give yourself time to settle and then look for consistency. A happy and grounded individual will be relatively consistent in their moods and the way that they treat you. Just give that a thought for a minute and let it settle. Who has this consistent trait in your life? Do you actually have anyone in your life with this trait? I can honestly say that a decade ago I was surrounded by the inconsistent energies of people I was consistently trying to please. After letting them all go (itself not an easy task especially with close family) and after realising that they would not change; my happiness and moods have been more level and consistent than I could have ever dreamed off.

I have witnessed the Agent acting as 'agent provocateur'. If your primary directive, your training and mission is observation and non-intervention but your (self-appointed) communal role is to help fight injustice and keep a balance of sorts, how can there be no intervention? The answer is actually very simple. Lead them to water but do not drown them in your moral hypocrisy. I have fallen for this trap of thinking 'I am the more trustworthy and moral so I will judge the world'. Try an approach that is aligned to the sufferers. Instead of helping others for self-enhancement try and do it anonymously and your karma will pay dividends believe me.

The major warning signs of an Agent are:

Manipulative: either directly or through others with some evident satisfaction.

Dishonest: The easy lies that take advantage or get them out of trouble.

Irresponsible: Failing to meet work and financial obligations.

Impulsive: Making big life altering decisions without prior planning. Also prone to outburst of rage or aggression. I have seen this behaviour from Agents at their dogs and even their own children.

Disregard of others: The rights and feelings of others are inconsequential and sometimes openly so and may be admitted in jest (making jokes about their own questionable morals is a common theme).

Remorseless: A constant rationalisation for negative actions. A true belief that they are in the right and others are to blame for the Agents abuse.

They are 'self-aware': They may know they function and think differently to others.

They struggle with empathy: Sometimes admittedly. You may witness that they have difficulty making meaningful relationships that are anything other than skin deep, or to further their social position.

They may mistake quiet strength for emotional detachment. This could be the Agent's chance to fill this supposed weak spot within your energy so you become reliant on them and bend to their whims. I have had a few Agents try and work their dark magic on me with this intent. I must admit I am so accustomed to it now that sometimes I play along just to see how far they are willing to go. It is usually further than you think (or would be comfortable with). I would not advise playing these games with Agents unless you have a strong Will and are well versed in protecting yourself from manipulation.

They may misinterpret your independence for arrogance, you know you are happy in your own skin. You are doing your shadow work and know that you will always be working on yourself. An Agent will see their weakness through your strength and will be threatened by this. Success sparks jealousy and these are the kind of people who will target you. Initially there may offer their services or friendship. You may notice that the people that surround them have absolutely no idea who this Agent really is. You can 'see' them. As the quiet observer you know that they are not as they pretend to be.

But how do we remove these people from our lives if they are not going to change?
Everybody changes daily, it makes me smile inside when I bump into a long lost friend who says 'you haven't changed a bit'. Our physical body is in constant change. Although it does take 7-10 years, every single cell in our body is replaced. Physically you are completely different

to who you were a decade ago. Psychologically (or psychospiritually) you change as well. I have lost and gained many different personality traits over the years. Some take more work to let go of, especially the ones that give us a feeling of strength even when they could harm others. People can change, it is more a case of whether they feel the need to.

You can't change Agents and you shouldn't. Protect yourself from them, learn how to read peoples energy and if they are consistently manipulative, never let your guard down. Do not take anything they say personally. If they say you look ill do not believe them. If they say 'you're not a writer, you can't publish a book', throw that energy back, say 'thanks for your support, I'm sure people will read it…'

Always pause for thought when they ask you a question, it will blindside them and says 'you do not control me or this conversation'. Take back your power. We are all just as important as each other. It is not your job to make others happy or to tell them how great they are to gain there support. Some Agents may not know what real love or friendship actually is. As I have said before: subtle manipulations and mind games are not your playground, be honest with your words and your intentions.

Agents will try to get you in a psychospiritual position where they can do their best damage.

However, if being around certain people makes you irritable I would advise you to remember that when people trigger us it is usually because we are uncomfortable witnessing the dark sides of them that may also belong within ourselves…

"Do not judge, or you too will be judged. For in the same way you judge others, you will be judged, and with the measure you use, it will be measured to you again". Matthew 7:1-5. Even the Bible knew that what goes around comes around.

The greatest weapon against deceptive behaviour is a highly vibrational person. They possess a lie detecting ability that is finely tuned to pick up discrepancies in energetic, emotional and physical behaviours. This is not necessarily a learnt skill or ability, but a direct consequence from a life of spiritual work and honing emotional intelligence (not everyone who practices spirituality is emotionally intelligent). Whether they are yogis, energy healers, Reiki masters, whatever and however they practice, simply being in this higher vibrational state for a long period of time gives them great power and intuition.

This makes interactions with these spiritual folk (by Agent's and other deceptor's that thrive on half-lies and manipulation) very uncomfortable indeed. Any deception or false pretence is made aware in their presence and even to other onlookers who may have been deceived otherwise. In this sense, the mere arrival of a highly vibrational person is the catalyst for change; the torch in the dark that illuminates our issues, not just the Agents, but everybody's.

This is why we find some people intimidating but essentially honest. If you try to lie to these souls, you will stumble over your words or feel inexplicably nervous.

The seeming innocence of their kind questions have the potential to unravel an Agents lies but in a way where the Agent will confess themselves. They do not have to ask the tough questions but are capable of doing so with compassion, without any fierce energy behind their words. This honest compassion is dishonesties kryptonite.

If you are an Agent, I highly recommend not attacking one of these spiritual beings. The karmic lessons will come hard and fast. You will not be destroyed but your life (and this version of your ego) will be forced to change very quickly in order for quick and hard lessons to be learnt. This karmic rebound will attack you personally, it will happen whether your innocent target knows you are attacking them or not. We all suffer karma but highly vibrational people work with it daily, they have a natural defence and a strong understanding of the karmic system. They have the ability to speed the process of karma in order to move through its lessons without stagnation and repetition.

As uncomfortable as this can feel, try to see it as a unique opportunity for growth and honesty. By removing our deceptive public facades we can start to work on and love what lies beneath them. I have come across these light bringers before and they often feel dark and light at the same time, they often feel deep because we may be shallow. If you spend long enough in reciprocal mentorship with them, if you do the work and its becomes your way of being; you will gain this ability to balance the energy of others around you, without any effort or loss of your own.

If you have read this, can see this behaviour in yourself and want some help to stop it then please reach out to a health care professional or if you are more spiritually inclined a holistic therapist or counsellor will help you get to the roots of the problem.

I still see parts of the Agent within myself from time to time. When you become aware of these behaviours, when you become the 'witness' you take away power from that which you observe.

What the world needs now more than ever is transparency.

Good luck on your wisdom journey, peace and love to you all…

And to those I have been brave enough to leave behind: 'The peace I feel without your presence in my life is worth being the villain in your story' - Sheldon Cameron

Conclusion For Now

"Don't let yourself forget how many doctors have died, furrowing their brows over how many deathbeds. How many astrologers, after pompous forecasts about others' ends. How many philosophers, after endless disquisitions on death and immortality. How many warriors, after inflicting thousands of casualties themselves. How many tyrants, after abusing the power of life and death atrociously, as if they were themselves immortal.

How many whole cities have met their end: Helike, Pompeii, Herculaneum, and countless others.

And all the ones you know yourself, one after another. One who laid out another for burial, and was buried himself, and then the man who buried him - all in the same short space of time.

In short, know this: Human lives are brief and trivial. Yesterday a blob of semen; tomorrow embalming fluid, ash.

To pass through this brief life as nature demands. To give it up without complaint.

Like an olive that ripens and falls.

Praising its mother, thanking the tree it grew on."

- Marcus Aurelius, <u>Meditations</u>

To be able to write is a precious gift. I truly hope that everyone who is able and willing does some form of journalling or creative writing to try and make sense of this soup that we learn and grow within.

I hope this book has helped you, either by triggering you and therefore given you a chance to feel into your 'dark necessities' or by inspiring you.

I am a product of my environment and I consistently adapt to and manipulate my surrounding in order to try and lead a peaceful, balanced existence. I have children and animals that I feed and nurture and I truly, deeply love living.

If I wrote this again (and I might) in ten years time; the chapters would be different, my perspective would have changed but the underlying theme of imbalance would remain. I believe I may just express them from a more conservative viewpoint.

Humans are incredibly resilient and (although this book may suggest otherwise) we are an optimistic race. With all of the chaos of war and media, advertising and corruption; with all of the negative aspects of humanity, hope remains and Prometheus smiles upon us still.

We are people that have evolved and thrived in communities of a hundred or so souls. To live like we do today is unnatural. The release of technology that connects us directly to artificial intelligence will be the end of the Homo Sapien. We are witnessing a manmade evolution, the beginning of something that will evolve so fast it will be unrecognisable within months and it will not stop there. There are many reasons why my family moved to the Highlands in 2024, but you cannot fully escape the system anymore, not on this planet. There are satellites over every single part of the Earth and soon there will be self-sufficient drones as well.

I have managed to escape certain parts of the 'rat race' but council tax and energy bills keep us (as a family) rooted in the system. We do not fight the laws that protect peoples rights, we oppose any form of control that subjects us and our family to a possible dystopia. The British government is making it harder and harder for us 'Highlanders' to live this rural life. They do not even supply working gritters in Sutherland in the Winter… We still pay our taxes. The Crown does not provide acceptable vehicles for the Royal Mail, but we still pay tax towards the Post Office Network and are subject to Royalist propaganda. The schools are falling apart physically and academically but we still pay our taxes. It is fairly obvious they would rather we were in major cities under watchful eyes and costing less money. Only the Gods know where the bastards spend this money, it is the eternal joke that remains unanswered.

The only way I see 'them' getting up here in this wild part of the Highlands is with drones. Unfortunately, the technology is already theirs. You can scoff and laugh all you like, it will happen and you will either bow down or fight, expose each other or unite. The choice is yours. Educate yourself and question everything you are ever told. Do not for one minute trust any government institutes and religions that suggest further reading outside of their approved list is scandalous or sinful. Most importantly, accept each others differences. We are not living life as a hive mind, we are here to experience everything in its ambiguity. Enjoy it, but "let's keep an eye on all our enemies while we're popping the champagne. Cause that's the thing about a victory; It comes in waves." - Dawes.

ADDITIONAL
HELP

Four Direction Blessings

Many people call in the four directions and also all there is above and below (Father Sky and Mother Earth).

We do this before a ceremony or healing as a means of grounding our souls and our bodies in this Earthly plain and recognising where we exist in the map of the cosmos.

It is also suggested that the advent of agriculture meant that the human race started to use tools such as the four directions to understand the seasons, the sun and its movements, day and night.

Here are some examples of blessings that we perform in ceremony and at personal alters. Please use them and adapt them in your own way.

An Exercise to Call in the Directions

Stand and face East. Close your eyes and place your hands on your heart. As you focus your imagination on the East and the rising sun, what feelings emerge for you.

Turn South and let your imagination soak in the qualities that come to you associated with the South.

Face West and take a deep breath and exhale. In your mind's eye, see and feel the sun setting. What associations does this bring to you?

Next, face North and observe how you feel in your heart. What meaning does the North hold for you?

In some cultures, the direction of Below is greeted to honour Earth.

And the direction of Above is welcomed to honour Sky.

Lastly, the direction of Within is acknowledged to honour the power of spirit and divine light that resides in each us.

Blessings to the Four Directions

The Blessing to the Four Directions has its roots in Native American culture. It is the belief that human beings are tied to all things in nature. It is this belief which assigned virtues to the four cardinal directions; East, South, West and North.

Blessing to the Four Directions 1

In times past it was believed that the human soul shared characteristics with all things divine. It is this belief which assigned virtues to the cardinal directions; East, South, West and North. It is in this tradition that a blessing is offered in support of this ceremony.

Blessed be this union with the gifts of the East. Communication of the heart, mind, and body. Fresh beginnings with the rising of each Sun. The knowledge of the growth found in the sharing of silences.Blessed be this union with the gifts of the South. Warmth of hearth and home. The heat of the heart's passion. The light created by both to lighten the darkest of times.

Blessed be this union with the gifts of the West. The deep commitments of the lake. The swift excitement of the river. The refreshing cleansing of the rain. The all encompassing passion of the sea.

Blessed be this union with the gifts of the North: A Firm foundation on which to build. Fertility of the fields to enrich your lives. A stable home to which you may always return.

Each of these blessings from the four cardinal directions emphasises those things, which will help you build a happy and successful union. Yet they are only tools. Tools, which you must use together, in order to create what you seek in this union.

Blessing to the Four Directions 2

In many ancient religious traditions, it is customary to bring a service of worship or celebration by calling on the four directions.

This is a way of symbolically inviting all of creation to be present and take part in the festivities.

This morning, we, too, want to invite the whole of creation to be with us here and now.

Oh Great Spirit of the North, we come to you and ask for the strength and the power to bear what is cold and harsh in life.

We come like the buffalo ready to receive the winds that truly can be overwhelming at time.

Whatever is cold and uncertain in our life, we ask you to give us the strength to bear it. Do not let the Winter blow us away.

Oh Spirit of Life and Spirit of the North, we ask you for strength and for warmth.

Oh Great Spirit of the East, we turn to you where the sun comes up, from where the power of light and refreshment come.

Everything that is born comes up in this direction the birth of babies, the birth of the puppies, the birth of ideas and the birth of friendship.

Let there be the light.

Oh Spirit of the East, let the colour of fresh rising in our life be glory to you.

Oh Great Spirit of the South, spirit of all that is warm and gentle and refreshing, we ask you to give us this spirit of growth, of fertility, of gentleness.

Caress us with a cool breeze when the days are hot.

Give us seeds that the flowers, trees and fruits of the Earth may grow.

Give us the warmth of good friendships.

Oh Spirit of the South, send the warmth and the growth of your blessings.

Oh Great Spirit of the West, where the sun goes down each day to come up the next, we turn to you in praise of sunsets and in thanksgiving for changes.

You are the great colored sunset of the red West, which illuminates us.

You are the powerful cycle, which pulls us to transformation.

We ask for the blessings of the sunset.

Keep us open to life's changes.

Blessing to the Four Directions 3

Long ago, people believed the human soul shared characteristics with all things celestial.

They therefore designated virtues to the East, South, West, and North.

So, in keeping with that age-old tradition . . .

We bless this marriage with the virtues of the East: communication between your hearts, minds, and bodies; fresh beginnings with the rising of every day's Sun; and the value of the wisdom of sharing silences.

We bless this marriage with the virtues of the South: a warm and welcoming home; the delight of your hearts' passion; and the ability of both to lighten the darkest of times.

We bless this marriage with the virtues of the West: the deepness of the lake; the swift flow of the river; the newness after rain; and the all-encompassing fervor of the sea.

We bless this marriage with the virtues of the North: a firm foundation to enrich your lives; a constant home to which you will always return.

Each of these blessings emphasises things that will help you build a happy and successful marriage.

But remember, they are only tools; tools you must both use — individually and together, in order to have what you seek from this marriage.

Let the image of water and the romance of your story always flow in your hearts in strong waves, knowing they are guiding you towards a goal fulfilled, a dreaming that is true.

Blessing to the Four Directions 4

Great Spirit of Light, come to me out of the East with the power of the rising sun.

Let there be light in my words, let there be light on my path that I walk.

Let me remember always that you give the gift of a new day.

And never let me be burdened with sorrow by not starting over again.

Great Spirit of Love, come to me with the power of the North.

Make me courageous when the cold wind falls upon me.

Give me strength and endurance for everything that is harsh, everything that hurts, everything that makes me squint.

Let me move through life ready to take what comes from the north.

Great Life-Giving Spirit, I face the West, the direction of sundown.

Let me remember everyday that the moment will come when my sun will go down.

Never let me forget that I must fade into you.

Give me a beautiful colour, give me a great sky for setting, so that when it is my time to meet you, I can come with glory.

Great Spirit of Creation, send me the warm and soothing winds from the South.

Comfort me and caress me when I am tired and cold.

Unfold me like the gentle breezes that unfold the leaves on the trees.

As you give to all the Earth your warm, moving wind, give to me, so that I may grow close to you in warmth.

Celtic 4 Directions

East - Air

South - Fire

West - Water

North - Earth

My Morning Prayer

This is how I ground myself from day to day. Every morning before I start to write (after I have let our wolf pack outside for their own rituals), these short prayers set me up in spirit and mind. I use white sage to cleanse my alter and my body during the 'Affirmation'. I try and feel the words not just say them. I am sharing this because, although it is personal, it has been very rewarding . It can be changed in any way to suit your beliefs or lack thereof. It is just an example of what a spoken meditation can look like.

I perform this in the order below, it flows best for me this way. Enjoy.

Prayer for Abundance

We have so much before us and for this we are thankful. We have so many blessings, and for this we are thankful.

There are others not so fortunate, and by this we are humbled.

We shall make an offering in their name to the Gods who watch over us, that those in need are someday as blessed as we are this day.

4 Directions

I call the powers of the East. The spirits of the sun, of fire, light, illumination and creativity.

I call the spirits of the South. The spirits of water, the plant kingdom, of trust and flow.

I call the powers of the West. The spirits of Earth, of the deep, of introspection and our Earth dream.

I call the spirits of the North. The spirits of air, of our relations the animals, of wisdom and discernment.

I call all there is above and all there is below and Great Spirit to be with me and support me during this day. I pray that whatever I do and create is for the higher good of all life.

Affirmation:

I release all energies that do not serve me.

I release any worries from my body and my home.

I release all my conditioned patterns and I trust the Universe and my intuition to guide me.

Daily Mantra

I am connected to source.

I am connected to my higher self.

I am directly connected to all that there is and all that there ever will be.

I have the power to manifest and I use it for the betterment of myself and all beings.

I am loving awareness.

"Show me what I need to know for today".

Closing

Mar a bha, mar a tha, mar a bhitheas gu brath, ri tragadh 's ri lionadh.

Correct pronunciation is not easy to find on the internet, if you know a Scottish or Irish person who speaks Gaelic they will should be able to help you. If not the English is as follows:

"As it was, as it is, as it shall ever be, with the ebb and with the flow."

Blessed be/So may it be/So it is required/So mote it be etc.

The Author

This is where you'll find me. On the land with the animals, with our three children and always outside whatever the weather. Fishing for mackerel from our boat and pollock from the Bay, tending to the sheep, writing, home educating ('unschooling') or healing clients.

We have done a complete 180° on our lives. It was planned for years but only possible on remote contracts. Kate and I moved our then 2 children to Badcall Bay in February of 2024. Only a year later we now have a growing number of sheep, a puppy, 15 chickens and another beautiful girl. Our family has grown and so have we.

Ethical living is not easy in a town. You will be surprised to hear that it is even harder here in the relative wilderness. In some ways we have taken a step backwards. We bulk order from ethical online shops, but

The view of Quinag from our croft

with high courier charges and lack of local sources it is expensive and intermittent. We are slowly finding a rhythm and that is the key...

Slowing down... not feeling guilty when the weather takes your working day away from you. Breathing in the fresh sea air and drinking the peat brown Lochan water. Having gratitude every moment of every day that we live in the land of the Gods.

This place is the source of my inspiration. The land and the weather are unavoidable and ethereal in their power

and beauty. You cannot tame nature here, no amount of human manipulation can stop the howling winds or calm the crystal clear waters.

Interactions with the local community provide an ample source of material. Just because the villages are smaller does not mean their characters are. In fact, they are more obvious here and more hardy. The outsiders are drawn to living a wild existence. Some have come to escape and are finding their own rhythm.

The land has welcomed us and we are grateful, honest and consistent in our interactions with it and the locals.

With our retreat in its planning stages, we have a holistic writing retreat and and a course in Animism in the making.

We welcome anyone, spiritual or not to our land. For our healing help or just to let the land and space to do its work. This is where I go to heal, I just never leave!

With two glamping pods in place and four off-grid large insulated yurts coming to our Croft complete with school and yoga tent; our plans are slowly starting to come together. Healing is our main focus. Hand fasting, ceremonies, meditations, drumming circles and when we are ready we will pass on some of our wisdom through courses. We will keep our little haven, small, warm and welcoming.

For more information please visit our website www.badcallbayretreat.com. You can contact us from this page. Please reach out if you want to come and visit or discuss this book.

Acknowledgments

First of all my favourite Medicine Woman, my wife Katie. Without you I would still be propping up the bars (if allowed) in the town where we first met. You are my best friend, my greatest human ally. I love our journey with its ebbs and flows. Long may it last monkey.

My children: Pandora, Wolf and Takaya. You brighten dark Highland days and bring me down to Earth by just being your magical selves. My patience teachers and fire bringers. My real loves.

My dogs: Ava, Teddy, Maximus and Lois. Your unlimited love, patience and friendship will never be forgotten. Thank you for keeping me company and warming my feet with my 5am starts.

My mentors: Jay & Kestrel Oakwood, Sandra Ingerman, Stephen Mulhearn, Andrew Cooper-Knight and all of the wise souls that have helped me learn and shown me the importance of working with my shadow self, my dark necessities.

My friends: You know who you are. Our humble friendships have given me peace and restored my faith in the human race. Keep shining your lights, together we will do our bit to bring the balance back.

My guides and Gods: Without your guidance and hard lessons I would not have the courage to face my fears, to be the honest man I strive to be. Our journey is an infinite one, I look forward to meeting you in Spirit. Please be gentle!

My 'angle on the tube'. I hope you have had a full life and are still living, learning and bringing joy through connections.

Further Reading

Not in any particular order but in the order they come to mind. All off the following have helped me on my journey so far…

A New Earth - Eckhart Tolle

The Four Agreements - Don Miguel Ruiz

The Fifth Agreement - Don Miguel Ruiz & Don Jose Ruiz

Fire In The Head - Tom Cowan

Odin's Gateways - Katie Gerrard

Galdrbok - Nathan J Johnson & Robert J Wallis

Winds Of Spirit - Renee Baribeau

The Ways Of The Lonely Ones - Manly Hall

Tao Te Ching - Cao-Hsiu Chen

The Soul Retrieval Journey - Sandra Ingerman

Walking In The Light - Sandra Ingerman

Medicine For The Earth - Sandra Ingerman

The Way Of The Shaman - Michael Harner

The Eden Conspiracy - Paul Wallis

Ani.Mystic - Gordon White

The Tibetan Book Of The Dead - Graham Coleman

A Book Of Pagan Prayer - Ceisiwr Serith

The Untethered Soul - Michael A Singer

Animal Spirit Guides - Steven D. Farmer

Women Who Run With Wolves - Clarissa Pinkola Estés

Three Waves Of Volunteers And The New Earth - Dolores Cannon

The Shamans Body - Arnold Mindell

Psychic Empath Abilities - Willow Kumar

The Alchemist - Paulo Coelho

The Lakota Way - Joseph M Marshall

Black Elk Speaks - John G Neihardt

Haste Ye Back!

Printed in Great Britain
by Amazon

57598481R00129